BRENDAN MURRAY

The youngest of five children, Brendan grew up in Salford, Lancashire before training as an actor and working for ten years in TIE, fringe, Rep and commercial theatre. From 1982 to 1985 he was Head of Education at the Belgrade Theatre Coventry and in 1989/90, writer-in-residence at the Crucible Theatre Sheffield – where his playwriting career really began. Since then he has divided his time between writing, directing and teaching, principally at Drama Studio London. In 2002/3 he was the Visiting Gulbenkian Fellow in the Department of Palliative Care & Policy at King's College Hospital and, from 2003 to 2008, Artistic Director of Oxfordshire (Touring) Theatre Company.

He's written for many of the leading small scale and young people's theatre companies in the UK as well as well as the Sherman Theatre, Cardiff and the Royal Exchange Theatre, Manchester.

His plays – of which there are over thirty for people of all ages – have been produced throughout the UK and abroad. *How high is Up?* has had over twenty productions worldwide and been translated into German, Welsh, Spanish and Serbian! *Big Baby* was shortlisted for the John Whiting Award in 2000; *Eliza's House* (published by Samuel French) won the Arts Council Children's Award (now known as the Theatre Centre Brian Way Award) in 2001, and *Scarlet Ribbons* won The Writers' Guild of Great Britain Award (for which he has been shortlisted on several occasions) in 2009.

Like the good northerner he is, he lives in Brighton and you can find out more about him at **www.brendanmurray.co.uk**

First published in the UK in 2013 by Aurora Metro Books
67 Grove Avenue, Twickenham, TW1 4HX
www.aurorametro.com info@aurorametro.com
The Falling Sky © 2013 Brendan Murray
Missing In Action © 2013 Brendan Murray
Entertaining Angels © 2013 Brendan Murray
Introduction © 2013 Brendan Murray
In-house editors: Rebecca Gillieron and Cheryl Robson
Cover Design © 2013 Alice Marwick www.alice-marwick.co.uk

With thanks to: Martin Gilbert, Simon Smith, Neil Gregory, Richard Turk, Alex Chambers, Ziallo Gogui, Joanne Bircsak, Imogen Facey.

10 9 8 7 6 5 4 3 2 1

Printed by Good News Digital, London, UK
ISBN: 978-1-906582-18-0

BIG THEATRE IN SMALL SPACES

by
Brendan Murray

The Falling Sky

Missing in Action

Entertaining Angels

AURORA METRO BOOKS

For

Jessie at Upton Village Hall and village halls everywhere: the people who run them; the people who use them and the people who make theatre in them.

CONTENTS

INTRODUCTION

How I got here from there...

Just call me David Hare. Or maybe, not. Maybe David Hare wouldn't like it. Come to think of it, maybe I wouldn't like it either. Let me explain...

Back in 1989 when David Hare was beginning his trilogy of plays for the National Theatre, (*Racing Demons, Murmuring Judges* and *The Absence of War*) about the Church of England, the British legal system and British political parties, I was just starting out as a solo playwright after ten years as an actor/deviser/director. And just as I'd spent those years working not on the great stages of London and Stratford but in studio theatres and school halls, so the people who now asked me to write plays for them were not running the National Theatre or the RSC but rather small theatre companies working with and for young people and local communities.

Over the next fifteen years I wrote for Theatre Centre, Red Ladder, The Sherman Theatre Cardiff, Solent Peoples Theatre, Greenwich & Lewisham YPT, Blackpool Youth Theatre, Jersey Arts Centre, The Unicorn and the Studio of the Royal Exchange. The briefs varied widely but all the plays were designed to be entertaining, relevant and accessible to audiences who might not be regular theatre-goers.

In 2003, I became Artistic Director of Oxfordshire (Touring) Theatre Company. OTTC did exactly what it said on the tin: it toured theatre to venues throughout Oxfordshire and beyond. Not big venues like theatres or Arts Centres but small venues like residential homes and village halls. The work was mostly new, not without ambition, and tailored to predominantly rural audiences who might otherwise – individually or collectively – find it difficult to access live theatre.

The Falling Sky

When I'd been at OTTC for a year or so, I started to wonder about making a show not only *for* our rural audiences but also *about* them. What got me thinking was the furore that had surrounded the passing of the Hunting Act 2004 – a piece of legislation given more Parliamentary time than the decision to invade Iraq. What's more, I had two friends – a country boy and a city girl but both animal lovers – on opposite sides of the argument. I wondered why fox hunting was such an emotive and divisive issue and how much it mattered to people in rural communities. So I decided to find out.

For three months or so I interviewed just about anyone who would talk to me: dairy farmers, land agents, entrepreneurs, young mums, old people at lunch clubs, children, teenagers, anyone. They talked about all sorts of things: the demise of small farms; affordable housing, loss of local amenities (schools, shops, pubs) and, yes, fox hunting. But what seemed to underpin everything was a feeling of disempowerment; a feeling that people in cities (London in particular) were making decisions about rural life when they knew (or cared?) very little about it. And people resented this.

From the stories people told me – and the people themselves – *The Falling Sky* developed over the next two years and eventually toured (locally and nationally) in autumn 2007. With its exceptional cast and production, the show was one of the most talked about in the company's twenty-five year history. I was asked after one performance if we changed the script every night. 'No,' I replied, 'why do you ask?' 'Because that was about *our* village. I know those people. They live here.'

As well as generating a deal of debate in the villages where it played, *The Falling Sky* also, in a way, gave rise to the other two plays in this volume as among the people who saw it were Mary Swann, Artistic Director of Proteus Theatre and Daniel Buckroyd (then Artistic Director of New Perspectives Theatre). Mary was wondering about how military life affects Service personnel and their families and Daniel asked me if I'd be interested in writing a play about the position of the Church of England in rural communities. Knowing next to nothing about either topic, I immediately agreed to both proposals.

Missing In Action

Following a similar *modus operandi* to *The Falling Sky*, I started reading and watching documentaries about military life but, above all, I talked to people at the sharp end.

I wanted to know everything: why people joined up, about their training, how they felt when deployed and – from the families' perspective – to understand what it's like to see someone you love experience the ups and downs of Service life. The stories people told me were touching, terrifying, humorous and humbling. For many, Service life had been a time of pride and comradeship and bravery. But for some – and often these were the same people – there had also been a price to pay and they had paid with life or limb or peace of mind. Indeed, many of people I spoke to had not only been traumatised by their experiences but left with their resulting post traumatic stress unrecognised and untreated.

In the UK, we're brilliant at training people to fight on our behalf, turning often unfocussed civilians into highly motivated, professional soldiers, sailors and airmen and women. But we're not so good at equipping these people for their return to civvy street. Even without exposure to any particularly traumatic experience this can be a difficult transition but given the terrible nature of some of the things they witness and undergo, the sad truth is that many ex-Service men and women are fighting long after they have retired from the Military, against the terrors that haunt them still, the stigma of mental illness, and the reluctance of society to help them in their struggle.

Using personal testimony perhaps even more than the other plays in this volume, *Missing In Action* tells the story of two young soldiers and their families: how one dies in combat and how the other lives on to fight a personal war of survival long after his time in the Military. It's sobering to reflect that one in four homeless people is a former member of the armed services, over 20,000 veterans are in prison or on probation, and more Falklands' veterans have taken their own lives in the past thirty years than died in the original conflict. Post Traumatic Stress Disorder (PTSD) is not going away and cannot – must not – be ignored.

Entertaining Angels

New Perspectives Theatre Company tours to regional towns and cities; to venues in London – even New York – but predominantly (like Oxfordshire Touring and Proteus) it tours to villages all over England. Go to any of these villages and I'm willing to bet you'll find a church: still at the centre of things geographically but what about in other respects?

Just as I interviewed lots of service personnel and their families in preparation for *Missing in Action* so, for *Entertaining Angels,* I spoke to church ministers and their partners, church wardens, lay readers, believers, agnostics, atheists, anyone really who had something to say about the Church's place in contemporary rural life. The resulting play – *Entertaining Angels* – is, on one level, the story of the relationship between a particular vicar and his parish. But it also wonders about wider social and religious matters: the pressures that priesthood puts on a marriage, what it might mean to call yourself a Christian, and if and when we should draw the line in our attempt to follow Christ's example of loving our neighbour.

This Anthology

As you'll see if you read all the plays in this volume, they share not only their research-based roots but also certain thematic elements (principally, I suppose, that of personal and social responsibility) – not to mention something of a penchant for pregnancy tests and vagrants! *The Falling Sky* has already had a successful second production and I hope all the plays might find a home both in professional theatres and on the amateur stage – anywhere in fact, that people are interested in accessible, challenging, character-based drama.

When I came to look at them as a collection (for the purposes of this anthology) I realised that here indeed were three 'state of the nation' plays albeit ones that look at the world from a decidedly domestic perspective and designed initially for rural venues.

So maybe not David Hare after all (I suppose that's BIG THEATRE IN BIG SPACES) but rather *Big Theatre in Small Spaces.*

Brendan Murray

THE FALLING SKY

THE FALLING SKY

Commissioned by Oxfordshire (Touring) Theatre Company and first performed at Upton Village Hall on March 6th, 2005 with the following cast:

CHARACTERS

Patience Dodds, a widow	Hazel Maycock
Sally Armstrong, a farmer's wife	Kate Adams
David Haworth, a landowner	Richard Walker
Caroline Bishop, an incomer	Carol Fitzpatrick
John, a man of the land	Stephen Middleton

Director	Clare Smout
Designer	Keith Baker
Artistic Director OTTC	Brendan Murray

Thanks: to all those who gave their time during the research; everyone who responded to the first draft; the staff at OTTC, the creative team and above all Clare, without whom…

PART ONE: SUMMER

Darkness: a bell tolls, far away...

JOHN   In the beginning God created the heavens and the earth. And the earth was without form and void: and darkness was upon the face of the deep. And God said: Let there be light. And there was light.

Dawn.

John with arms spread and eyes closed...

JOHN   So God created man in His own image: male and female, created He them. And God saw everything that He had made, and, behold: it was very good.

He opens his eyes and all sing:

ALL   As I walked out one midsummer morning
For to view the fields and the flowers so gay
'Twas there on the banks of the sweet primroses
That I beheld a most pleasant day.
I will go down to some lonely valley
No man on earth shall e'er me find
Where the pretty little birds do change their voices
And every moment shall blow boisterous winds.
Come all you maidens that go a-courting
Pray give attention to what I say
For there's many a dark and cloudy morning
Turns out to be a sun-shining day.

John goes.

Morris dancing music plays...

PATIENCE   Midsummer's day! Talk about time flying. Mind, spring was late this year: still had my heating on in May. Sometimes May's hot but not this year. This year it was miserable. But the weather's finally picking up. Warm and dry. But you don't want it too warm, do you? You can have too much of a good thing. And then it stops being a good thing, I find, and starts being a bad thing.

SALLY   I can't imagine not farming. On the farm where I grew up – my brother farms it now – we had a bit of everything: sheep, pigs, cows. I wanted my kids to have the same upbringing as me: space to run about; learn about animals. The thing about cows: they're individuals. You see one coming, you know who it is. Sheep... Well, sheep are more... Well, they're sheep, aren't they? You might know the odd troublemaker or sickly one but on the whole... No, I miss the cows. They were hard work but I miss them.

DAVID   I've travelled pretty widely in my time: twenty-two years in the Warwickshires; been all over the world one way and another and God knows there are some beautiful, beautiful places on this earth. But the English countryside on a summer's morning with the sun rising and the birdsong and the air sweet as hay: there's nothing to beat it.

CAROLINE We've been here now, must be nearly a month. It felt like the right time for a move. The past few years we've been pretty preoccupied, trying to start a family: IVF, the whole shebang. (*Beat*) I'd've been happy to adopt but Matt... He wanted kids just as much as me but he needed them to be his own. It was a blow, I can't pretend it wasn't, but marriage isn't about *me* or *you*, is it? It's about *us*. And for us, it wasn't an option.

PATIENCE I was a land girl – I'm from Birmingham originally – but my husband, Leslie, he was born here and his grandparents – this is what his mother told me – they walked here from Mayfield, driving the pigs along the road. 1905. You'd have a job to drive pigs along the road now! And the people who've moved in, they work in Birmingham, London – so you don't see them during the day: professors; all sorts. And house prices! There's a council house up the end; they're asking two hundred thousand! It's got its own driveway but even so.

SALLY   The people who move here – 'blow-ins' Keith calls them – they don't always fit; don't like the smells. Mind you, I don't like pigs. You know when the wind's up! That's the thing with intensive farming: you get all that manure and then you can't spread it cos of phosphates getting into the waterways, which is fair enough. But that's the pressure now, to specialise, cos the supermarkets tell you what they'll pay. And the prices are dropping: we're probably making half what we were fifteen years ago.

DAVID   In the old days the farmer was king. You dined on your own eggs and butter and rode off to market because there were other people doing the work. I'm not sure how much actual farming my grandfather ever did. Even in my father's day this place had oh, nineteen, twenty men working full-time. And the muck went on the land and the land fed the livestock. Now we're purely arable, rape and barley mostly, although we've diversified in other ways: sold the cottages; converted some of the old sheds for light industrial use. We do a bit of shooting – anything we can really to keep things going.

CAROLINE   The house is fantastic. It was the rectory at one time, exactly what we were looking for, and nothing to do as the people we bought it from had just about done everything: new kitchen, bathrooms – not to mention the pool, which makes it sound like something out of *Footballers' Wives* I know but... And the garden: a proper kitchen garden! And growing our own food is something I really want to do. Sustainability: from now on that's the name of the game.

PATIENCE   Some things are better: we've all had water laid on and proper flush toilets and you can't tell me that's not an improvement. But food's not what it was. I bought some cheese – just a bit of cheddar – and it's got a sticker on it: 'Allergy Advice: Contains milk'. Cheese! Mind, I'm not sure how much milk it did contain cos it tasted like soap. It was all right toasted, you know, grated and toasted. I put a bit of salad cream with it, mix it up. It does for a meal.

SALLY   To be honest – Keith knows this but we don't speak about it cos I do the accounts – the farm hasn't made a profit for a while. In his dad's day it was easier, with subsidies and that and then when we took over, we still had a dairy herd and we used to sell green top milk – you know, unpasteurised – and there was a real market for that; it was a good little earner. People wanted it. And then of course there's a rule saying we can't sell it any more in case of brucellosis. No one had ever got it but it was a rule. So we had to stop. That's when I started hairdressing part-time and now I'm doing that and making cakes of an evening. I do the farmer's markets; shows; that kind of thing. And if it wasn't for my cakes, we wouldn't have the farm at all. (*Goes*)

DAVID   But the hoops you have to jump through! There's nothing a farmer hates more than filling in forms and the trouble with Britain is we gold-plate every directive and follow the rules to the nth degree. And DEFRA! It used to be that people working for the Ministry were from rural backgrounds. Not any more. You get letters asking about the sex of your bulls! It's the same everywhere: we're losing the skills. We had a chap work for us, and he could walk a thirty acre field and tell you if there was a hare or not in that field. These people are vanishing.

CAROLINE   I'm not going to be one of those people you hear about who move to the country and complain about the cockerel crowing or the smells. I *want* to hear the cockerel; I *want*... Well, I might not want the smells but I don't mind them if they're natural. They go with the territory, don't they? No, I want to be part of things. Matt's probably a bit more circumspect but he's looking forward to the slower pace. He'll only be here weekends for the time being but long term the plan is to work from home like me.

PATIENCE   At the WI yesterday we had a new member. But three had died. (*Beat*) I called at the church to remember them but it was locked, I'd forgotten that. Mrs Winston: very quiet; hardly spoke really but very nice. Mrs Drew: I can't say I ever liked her much. I shouldn't say that, I know but she was a funny woman. She could be very...disapproving. They found her in the WC. I don't suppose she'd approve of that. And Mrs...Watshername: little woman came from Derby when her husband died... always cheerful... like a little bird I used to think... made a lot of jam. Fraser! Mrs Fraser. I don't know if her husband was Scottish. Stroke. Only seventy-nine. (*Beat*) I forget sometimes that I'm getting old. People talk about old people, I think: that's not me, how can it be? When yesterday I was running to school, swinging my satchel. (*Beat*) I was so proud of that satchel. Course, there'd be nothing in it except some bread and dripping. Or cold toast. I've not had cold toast for a long time. I used to like it. I might have some for my tea tonight. With some of Mrs Fraser's jam. (*Beat*) But you know, when I was walking back from the church yesterday, no one stopped or said hello.

SALLY   We've had someone shooting lambs. Once a week or so. First time it was four. Since then it's generally one or two. Just leave 'em. They must come at night or early morning. We've had the police over but what can they do? Bit of a mystery.

DAVID   Just before Chris went back this last time, we rode up by Higham Wood – first thing – and the mist was rising with the sun and we sat there for the longest time, just looking at the land. And then I said: One day, my boy, all this will be yours! And he looked at me in that rather quizzical fashion that always reminds me of his mother... and then his face broke into a smile and we both roared with laughter and raced each other back to breakfast! It's true though: it will be his one day, God willing. (*Beat*) I won the race by the way.

CAROLINE I don't miss London at all. It's so impersonal. People are afraid, I think. And the last few years with all the terrorist palaver and security... That's the trouble with security – have you noticed? – never seems to make you feel any more secure. I'd had enough. We've kept the flat, the little flat Matt had before we were married: we were renting it out but now he's back there. It's only a studio but it's just a place to sleep Monday to Friday. This is home now. (*Goes*)

Patience watches John dance. He finishes.

PATIENCE   Very nice, John.

JOHN   Shall I dance some more?

PATIENCE   Oh, I think that was plenty.

JOHN   Shall I sing, then?

PATIENCE   Another time, eh?

JOHN   To every thing there is a season and a time to every purpose under heaven.

PATIENCE   That's right.

JOHN   A time to be born and a time to die; a time to plant and a time to pluck up that which is planted.

PATIENCE   A time to sing and dance and a time to go home and have a cup of tea.

JOHN   No more, then?

PATIENCE   No. But it was very nice.

Patience and John go. Caroline in her garden.

CAROLINE   Maybe it's just being somewhere new; maybe you're bound to notice more but I walk into the garden here and just sit; listen: birds, or a squirrel moving in the branches. The other day I saw a fox. And the light sometimes; clouds; how wood rots; fungus: I want to eat it all up. Not the fungus, just the whole... everything. And stars! I lie on the lawn at night, counting them. Eat your heart out, Patrick Moore. I never thought – never felt so part of things before; such a sense of belonging; being alive; life.

She closes her eyes and inhales but when she opens them again John is there.

CAROLINE   Who are you? What do you want? (*Beat*) I'm asking you what you want. (*Beat*) What are you doing here? (*Beat*) If you don't tell me what you're doing I'm going to call –

JOHN   Behold I stand at the door and knock. If any man

hear my voice and open the door, I will come to him and sup with him and he with me.

CAROLINE What?

JOHN And I will give him the Morning Star.

CAROLINE (*beat*) The newspaper?

JOHN I John, who also am your brother and companion in tribulation... heard behind me a great voice
as of a trumpet saying, I am Alpha and Omega, the First and the Last... the beginning and the ending...

CAROLINE Look, I don't know who you are but–

JOHN I am he that liveth and was dead.

Pause.

CAROLINE Right... Well I'm sorry but you can't stay here.

JOHN Can't I?

CAROLINE This is my garden.

JOHN God's own earth.

CAROLINE Perhaps, but this bit of it happens to be in private hands.

JOHN (*beat*) He's got the whole world in his hands.

CAROLINE That's as maybe.

JOHN He's got you and me, sister, in his hands.

CAROLINE Please go.

JOHN He's got the iddy biddy baby -

CAROLINE I don't want to have to call the police.

JOHN Don't you?

CAROLINE No. So off you go, now.

JOHN Off I go?

CAROLINE Yes. Please don't be difficult about it.

JOHN I'm not being difficult.

CAROLINE But you're not going, are you?

JOHN Where shall I go?

CAROLINE Er... Where did you come from?

JOHN I come from the father.

CAROLINE What? (*Beat*) Oh, God.

JOHN Yes! Will you sing with me?

CAROLINE I don't think this is the time or the place for singing.

JOHN (*singing*) He who would valiant be
'Gainst all disaster,
Let him in constancy –

CAROLINE Do you want me to call the police?

JOHN Will they sing with me?

CAROLINE No. No, they won't.

John considers for a moment then continues...

JOHN (*sings*) Let him in constancy
Follow the Master.
There's no discouragement –

CAROLINE Please! Please stop that.

John stops singing. Pause.

JOHN How about some Jim Reeves?

CAROLINE No singing. Please. Just go.

JOHN (*makes to go, stops*) There was a man... whose name was John... He came unto his own and they received him not.

A moment of beauty. Then John takes down his trousers, pulls them up again and runs off.

CAROLINE (*after a time*) God!

She goes.

Patience at home.

PATIENCE Mrs Frazer's jam was lovely. I never have much luck with jam. I either boil it too much or I don't boil it enough – something – so it doesn't set and runs all over the shop or it sets that hard you can hardly get it out of the jar. Even Leslie used to struggle with my jam and he was never one to complain. Even when he was ill. Especially. (*Beat*) Great big feller... Like a child he was at the end: meek; meek and mild. *(The sound of dogs barking)* And now here's my landlord, come to check up on me.

DAVID Hello there, Patience. I've just come to check up on you.

PATIENCE Well, I'm doing all right.

DAVID Not too hot for you?

PATIENCE No, we could do with a bit of sunshine.

DAVID You're right. As ever.

PATIENCE I don't know about that. Will you have a toffee?

DAVID Better not.

PATIENCE You used to like them.

DAVID I'm in training.

PATIENCE Oh!

DAVID Sponsored walk for the church roof.

PATIENCE Oh, Sally was saying. But that's a way off yet.

DAVID Still... Has she got Keith involved?

PATIENCE No time apparently. And he could do with losing a bit of weight.

DAVID I hear they've had some trouble.

PATIENCE *(beat)* Oh, with the sheep, yes.

DAVID   Terrible.

PATIENCE   She's enough to worry about.

DAVID   Bernard?

PATIENCE   I think he misses Pat. *(Beat)* Yes. *(Beat)* It'll be twenty years for Leslie, Monday.

DAVID   Will it really?

PATIENCE   I still miss *him*. I mean – don't get me wrong – he did nothing in the house. I had to do everything, so I don't miss him that way. But companionship, someone to talk to...

DAVID *(beat. Perhaps he sits.)* Yes.

PATIENCE   Forty-two years working for your father. Course he was under Mr Daniels at first – you won't remember him, he had a wooden leg and his wife came from Shrewsbury but it was your father as always mattered to him: The Major. Ha! He could be a stickler, couldn't he? Army training, I suppose. Remember how he'd turn up out of the blue? Do you remember that?

DAVID   I do.

PATIENCE   One minute you're on your own-io; the next: there he'd be.

DAVID   Yes.

PATIENCE   Wanting to know what's what.

DAVID   I remember.

PATIENCE   And woe betide you if he caught you slacking.

DAVID   I don't imagine he caught Leslie slacking.

PATIENCE   Oh no, he was a worker, Leslie. *(Beat)* They planted the covers together, Leslie and your dad. For the birds. The young birds.

DAVID   That's right. *(Beat)* I'm afraid they've gone now.

PATIENCE   The birds?

DAVID   No, the covers. Rather in the way, I'm afraid, when we got the new combine.

PATIENCE   Progress.

DAVID   Something like that.

PATIENCE   Used to be grazing, hadn't it?

DAVID   Rape now. Oil seed rape. There's a big demand: fuel, cooking oil.

PATIENCE   Is that right?

DAVID   The supermarkets.

PATIENCE   I still use lard.

DAVID   Yes.

Pause.

The dogs bark and David makes to go...

DAVID   Well –

PATIENCE   And how's your Christopher?

DAVID   He's well. He's very well. He was home not long since.

PATIENCE   Oh, he should've called in.

DAVID   He says hello. You know how it is. Only here five minutes.

PATIENCE   Your wife must've been pleased.

DAVID   We both were.

PATIENCE   Do you remember when he was little and Leslie'd let him in the cab, you know, on the tractor? (*Beat*) Don't think you were supposed to know about that!

DAVID   He was always fond of Leslie. (*Pause*) Captain now.

PATIENCE   Captain! I bet he looks smart.

DAVID   Going abroad soon.

PATIENCE Not –?

DAVID Afghanistan, yes.

PATIENCE I don't know what we're doing in half these places.

DAVID It's peace-keeping mainly; reconstruction work.

PATIENCE Let's hope so.

DAVID Yes.

PATIENCE I'll say a prayer for him.

DAVID That's good of you. And now if everything's all right –

PATIENCE You met our new blow-ins yet? Well, I haven't met *him* myself but *she* seems very nice. At the rectory, who bought the rectory.

DAVID No, I haven't met them.

PATIENCE He works in investments, the husband, and she's something to do with journalism... a magazine – not one you'd read – economics... she did say. Anyway, she's very nice. Youngish. No children. Running me to town, Friday.

DAVID *(moving away)* Very good.

PATIENCE Will you take some strawberries?

DAVID I won't, thank you.

PATIENCE I don't know what to do with them, I've that many.

DAVID You should make some jam.

PATIENCE Yes, I should. You're right. Yes. I'll do that.

A 17ᵗʰ century execution. The sound of a crowd...

JOHN By natural birth all men are equally and alike born to like propriety, liberty and freedom. I think the poorest he that is in England hath a life to live as the greatest he. God gaveth the earth to all men equally and we protest the right to cultivate the common land so we might feed ourselves, our wives and children, without the need for servants or masters but where all shall labour and share in the fruits of their work.

And why any man should hunt me down and seek to stop my mouth with hangman's noose or musket shot when all I say is that God be in all creatures and that men should harken to Jesus within them I do not know.

But this I know: that Christ would have us working not for profit but the common good, in harmony with nature, acknowledging man's place in the order of creation and not insisting on being forever and in all ways its master.

I am an honest, true-bred, free-born English-man that never in his life did love a tyrant or fear oppressor and I rest the nation's true friend and hearty well-wisher while I have a drop of blood running in my veins. And may God have mercy on my soul.

The sound of the crowd becomes the noises of Sally's farmyard. Caroline enters.

CAROLINE Hello there!

SALLY Oh, careful: your shoes!

CAROLINE What? Oo... see what you mean... Never mind. It's just I saw the sign... about the eggs.

SALLY Oh, right. Passing through?

CAROLINE No, I've... We've just moved into the old rectory.

SALLY Very nice.

CAROLINE I hope so.

SALLY Lovely house.

CAROLINE Yes.

SALLY   Not that I know it, really. I mean I knew the people who were there before.

CAROLINE The Turners?

SALLY   No! No, they weren't here five minutes - don't think it suited them, country life – no, the Hamiltons. Not that we mixed much: bit grand for the like of us.

CAROLINE Well, you must come over: we're not grand.

SALLY   Oh, good.

CAROLINE Whenever you like.

SALLY   Yes, well don't hold your breath.

CAROLINE Sorry?

SALLY   We don't get a lot of time for...

CAROLINE The farm keeps you pretty busy.

SALLY   You could say that. So: eggs!

CAROLINE Oh, yes! Eggs.

SALLY   How many would you like?

CAROLINE Just half a dozen.

SALLY (*beat*) Right.

CAROLINE Or a dozen. Make it a dozen.

SALLY   You sure?

CAROLINE Absolutely. They are organic?

SALLY   Oh. No. Not as such. Is that all right? I mean, they're free-range – obviously. A bit too free-range some of the time.

CAROLINE Well, they look happy enough.

SALLY   Yes. Sometimes I think it might be nice: scratching about to your heart's content.

CAROLINE Are they a lot of work?

SALLY   No. The kids feed 'em before they go to school.

CAROLINE   How many have you got?

SALLY   Kids or chickens?

CAROLINE   Kids.

SALLY   Two. But it feels like more sometimes with my husband and his dad.

CAROLINE   You all live together?

SALLY   The farm still belongs to Bernard legally – my father-in-law – not that he does much these days.

CAROLINE   Still, a lovely old house.

SALLY   You should try living in it.

CAROLINE   But lots of character.

SALLY   Oh, character; yeah, it's got bags of that. Plus damp bedrooms and a wonky Aga.

CAROLINE   Right.

SALLY   How about you? *(Beat)* Kids.

CAROLINE   No. No, it's just me and my husband.

SALLY   Big place for two of you, the Rectory.

CAROLINE   I work from home – just three days a week – and Matt's planning to do the same. Well, that's the idea...

SALLY   You sure you want a dozen then, if it's just the two of you?

CAROLINE   Yes. Yes, I'll make something... a quiche... something. *(Sally fetches the eggs.)* If you want to use the pool any time...

SALLY   Oh!

CAROLINE   It's not very big.

SALLY   Talk of the village when the last lot had it built.

CAROLINE   Bring the children. Or send them over after

school if you'd like them out of your hair for an hour or two.

SALLY *(returning)* Don't tempt me.

CAROLINE I'd love it. Matt's away during the week.

SALLY That's kind of you.

CAROLINE No, really.

SALLY That'll be £1.50.

CAROLINE Oh, right. Right. Thanks... Can I ask you...? There was a man...

SALLY Yes?

CAROLINE In my garden.

SALLY Did he quote the Bible at you?

CAROLINE Yes.

SALLY That's John. And did he tell you they were after him?

CAROLINE Who?

SALLY Cromwell and the Roundheads.

CAROLINE No.

SALLY Or sometimes it's the squire's men.

CAROLINE Have we got a squire?

SALLY It's just his mind; the way his mind works. You met anyone else yet?

CAROLINE At the Post Office.

SALLY Rosemary.

CAROLINE She's got me volunteering on the shop side.

SALLY That's Rosemary.

CAROLINE And I've been along to the WI.

SALLY Oh, very good!

CAROLINE Well... I can't see the point of coming to live in the country – in a village – if you don't want to *live* there – here – if you see what I mean.

SALLY There's plenty don't – want to live here, I mean. Or maybe they do but they just don't want to join in things. Or they're only here weekends. *(Beat)* But you're keeping busy by the sound of things.

CAROLINE Oh, I'm loving it. *(Beat)* This John...

SALLY Did he...? *(She mimes taking down trousers.)*

CAROLINE Yes.

SALLY Welcome to Shepton.

They go.

John runs on, looks up at the sky.

Night falls.

PART TWO: AUTUMN

Darkness.

JOHN   The harvest is past. The summer ended and we are not saved.

Light.

ALL *(sing)* John Barleycorn's a hero bold as any in the land
For ages good his fame has stood and shall for ages stand
The whole wide world respect in him, no matter friend or foe
And where they be that makes so free, he's sure to lay them low
Hey, John Barleycorn; Ho, John Barleycorn;
Old and young thy praise has sung: John Barleycorn
To see him in his pride of growth, his robes are rich and green
His head is spread with prickly beard, fit nigh to serve the queen
And when the reaping time comes round and Johnny's stricken down
He'll use his blood for England's good and Englishmen's renown.
Hey, John Barleycorn; Ho, John Barleycorn;
Old and young thy praise has sung: John Barleycorn.

John runs off.

PATIENCE   Harvest Festival today so the church was full. All the kiddies bringing things. And Mrs Parker with her display: wheat, oats and barley this year. My mother used to put it in soup. Anything to fill you up. Well, there were six of us. I never cared for it. Not the taste so much as... Like dumplings: slimy. I'd do them for Leslie sometimes cos he liked them but he'd eat anything, he would: clean his plate with a piece of bread – yes, and his tongue if he thought I

33

wasn't looking. *(Beat)* How did I get onto that? Oh, yes: Mrs Parker's cornucopia: too much of a good thing. *(Beat)* Still, the hymns were nice.

SALLY   Keith can't always manage it but I take the kids to church, Sundays. It's how I was brought up and it's something I feel quite strongly about. I won't say it's a comfort. You could do without it sometimes but it's the only chance I get to see people in the village. Farmers these days can be very isolated: some weeks Keith won't see a soul. It's no life. People keep going because they don't want to be the first generation to sell up. But so many farms have gone. And it's not just farms: we lost one of the pubs. Luxury flats. A hundred and sixty thousand for one bedroom. What use is that to anyone round here?

DAVID   Trouble is, there are so many rules these days we've lost our common sense. One time, someone had measles, you'd all be trouped round there so you'd get it and get it over with. Now we vaccinate. There's this need to control; be in control; preserve everything as it might have been at some arbitrary – probably fictional – point in history. How do these people think villages ended up looking as they do? They weren't built like some kind of model development, they evolved over time. And if that evolution stops now we're done for: dead.

CAROLINE Well, so far so good. I mean I wish Matt could be here more – he seems to be busier than ever – but I'm really feeling part of things: helping with the parish newsletter; volunteering in the shop; having Sally's kids round. And I'm still managing to work... Not that it seems to matter as much these days: I mean obviously the growth of the Chinese economy is vitally important but what about the church roof appeal; and the threat to rural Post Offices and the size of my pumpkins?

PATIENCE Course I was never a church-goer before I got married. My father didn't approve. A lot of mumbo-jumbo he called it. But Leslie was always very God-fearing. I used to worry that I didn't believe everything I was supposed to but I don't worry about that now. *(Beat)* I worry about break-ins. And those kiddies in Africa, the ones you see on the news; people blown up; people being shot. And that young fella on the underground the other year... That was here. Sometimes it's hard to give thanks at all.

SALLY   All farmers want is a level playing field. If people would just buy British it would make a difference. And all the business with the Single Farm Payment – they took the old subsidies away – and fair enough, maybe it was time they did – but the computers couldn't deal with it. And meanwhile, we're getting bills for fertiliser, fodder, new stock. We've had to borrow. *(Beat)* There's been a lot of suicide in the more remote areas. For me, that's where the church comes in. But I worry about Keith sometimes. And then this business with the lambs...

DAVID   And the conservationists... They want to see you ploughing a field with a team of shire horses. Well, it's a nice idea but these people need to wake up to the realities of the commercial world. It's the supermarkets calling the shots now and everything has to be perfect. Does it taste of anything? Not really. But the consumer smiles and says nothing because it's buy-one-get-one-free: a bargain!

CAROLINE   They call it crop protection. Pesticides are what they mean: pesticides and fungicides and herbicides – yes, and fertilisers. And you know what's so clever about chemical fertilisers? They make the crop grow really fast but they reduce the plants' natural resistance so the farmer has to use all the other chemicals to compensate. You've got to hand it to the agro-chemical industry, it's brilliant: a perfectly engineered cycle of dependency. And the long-term effects of all this meddling? Nobody knows.

PATIENCE   Remembrance Day before you know it. I had an uncle die in the first war. Only seventeen. Before I was born – I'm not that old! – so I don't remember him but I do remember his name because when I was first married... I had a little boy but he was... It was a difficult labour; very long and he was stillborn... But we called him John after my uncle. And I like to think they're together somewhere, both going so young and being related and having the same name.

SALLY They'll be hunting again soon so that'll cause a stink. Most people round here couldn't really care one way or the other but it's a traditional country pursuit and I don't see what gives anyone the right to stop people doing it if that's what they enjoy.

DAVID I remember taking Chris out for the first time. He was so excited. Fearless too – at least until old Frank Dunmore bloodied him with the brush: he didn't care for that, thank you very much! But from then on it was something we did whenever we could. Something we shared: a passion.

CAROLINE I know we had a great summer but honestly I think it could've rained every day and I'd still be feeling positive. Just waking up here; the air; growing my own vegetables! It's everything I hoped it would be. And the village... The village is beautiful, perfect, peaceful...

A terrible sound of hounds and breaking glass.

David in Caroline's garden.

CAROLINE Oh, my God!

DAVID I'm most terribly sorry. *(Calling)* Kenny! Kenny!

CAROLINE What's going on?

DAVID I do apologise. I'm afraid our young fox has taken refuge in your greenhouse.

CAROLINE I don't quite –

DAVID And the hounds have followed. *(Calling)* Kenny, for God's sake!

CAROLINE But what are you doing in my garden?

DAVID As I say –

CAROLINE Is this a fox hunt?

DAVID   No, we don't start hunting till November. We're just cubbing today: training the young hounds.

CAROLINE   But you're chasing a fox.

DAVID   That's basically how the training works.

CAROLINE   I thought hunting was illegal now.

DAVID *(beat)* Well, not as such. Strictly speaking, hunting with dogs –

CAROLINE   But isn't that what you're doing?

DAVID   As I say, we're really only cubbing.

CAROLINE   There's a fox in my greenhouse; dogs running wild and a man on horseback on my lawn – if that's not hunting, I'd like to know what is.

DAVID   Yes. *(Beat)* It's probably a little late for this but perhaps I should introduce myself. David Haworth. I farm the Longton Estate.

Pause.

CAROLINE   Caroline Bishop.

DAVID   With hunting... it's exercising the horses. They love it, the dogs love it. It's not all about killing the fox.

CAROLINE   Really?

DAVID   You'd be amazed how often he gets away. *(Beat)* It's an emotive business, I know, but I'm sure you wouldn't object to rats being culled and the fox is vermin just the same. Oh he's pretty – I'll give you that – but he'll take a ewe – heavily in lamb – and eat its hind leg out. I've seen that. And pretty that certainly isn't.

CAROLINE   And hunting is the best way of controlling numbers?

DAVID   I'd say so, yes. There's snaring but personally I think that's cruel. You'll get animals trapped for days, they'll chew their own legs off to escape. That's the difference with hunting: the fox gets knocked off straight away. That's if we even catch him. There's no pain. One bite from a big dog, quick shake: dead.

CAROLINE   I've read the fox is torn to pieces.

DAVID   He's torn to pieces after, I admit, and that's not very pleasant but as I say, to me it's more about exercising the horses and dogs.

Glass breaking…

DAVID *(calling)* Kenny, will you call those young devils off! *(To Caroline)* I'm terribly sorry. They're not quite as biddable at this age as one would like. I assure you the cost of any damage will be covered.

CAROLINE   I'm not really worried about that.

DAVID   Even so –

CAROLINE   But what does concern me is a grown man chasing a defenceless animal with a pack of hounds.

DAVID   They're really only pups and the fox really does have to be controlled.

CAROLINE   Says who?

DAVID   Well, if you'll forgive me, says common sense.

CAROLINE   And does common sense say you can invade my garden?

DAVID   Absolutely not. I wouldn't dream of hunting over your land without permission. It's just with the fox holding up in your greenhouse and the young dogs being so excitable, I took the liberty of jumping the fence before they did any damage. *(Sound of breaking glass)* Kenny!

KENNY *(off)* Sorry, Mr Haworth. Oh, he's jumped through the bloody window! Go on, lads… He's off down towards the Bicester road.

DAVID   Well, it sounds as if the drama's over. If you let me know the cost of the glass…

CAROLINE   But what about –

DAVID   And labour, of course.

CAROLINE   I'm not talking about the greenhouse, I'm talking about the law.

DAVID   It's all rather complicated for the layman.

CAROLINE   Please don't patronise me.

DAVID   I wouldn't dream of doing so. Look, I know this must have been a dreadful shock – especially at this hour in the morning – but I can only apologise again.

Pause.

CAROLINE   Apology accepted.

DAVID   Thank you.

CAROLINE   Did you say you farmed the Longton Estate?

DAVID   Yes, along by the river and up to Higham Wood.

CAROLINE   So it's your men who have been doing all the spraying recently?

DAVID   Well...

KENNY *(off)* Mr Haworth!

DAVID   I'm being called.

CAROLINE   Yes.

DAVID   If you'll excuse me. *(He goes.)*

CAROLINE *(after a time)* Bloody cheek.

A 19th century courtroom...

JOHN   You are as well hung for a sheep as a lamb, they say, yet your Honour sends me to the colonies for no more than a rabbit. Do I admit my crime? How could I otherwise when I was taken with the rabbit in my coat? And yet to call it crime seems strange when it was done on land which once

I rented lawfully. But since the landlords so increased the rents we tenant farmers have been forced to seek a livelihood as labourers and that, in turn, denied to us at any wage a man could live by. And these same landlords who now enclose the fields by no other right than the say-so of their peers and cronies, reduce free men to wage slaves, forced to buy what once they grew. And why? Because they cannot bear to see folk live when they might profit more themselves. Did I take the rabbit? Yes, and I would take a hundred such to feed my wife and child who now, since my arrest, are thrown into the workhouse. And I condemned to seven years. And all this for a rabbit. And this now is the law in England. *(Beat)* God Save the Queen!

Patience at home with Sally…

PATIENCE   I've been feeling bad all day.

SALLY *(doing Patience's hair)* Oh?

PATIENCE   Not poorly. There's nothing wrong with me. Except my knees but you expect that at my age. And I used to love dancing. I'd rather go dancing than to the pictures. And I loved the pictures. Robert Donat, he was my favourite: a real gentleman. And Alan Ladd was very good. But very small, apparently. They had to stand him on a box when he was next to anyone. *(Beat)* Anyway, like I say, I'm not feeling very proud of myself.

SALLY   Why's that then?

PATIENCE   John came last night. I knew it was him. I can tell the way he knocks. And he was saying he'd something for me.

SALLY   What?

PATIENCE   I don't know cos I pretended not to be in. Mind, the lights were on and the curtains drawn so he could tell I was in. I suppose I could've been in the bathroom and not heard him but I did hear him. I heard him and I didn't answer. I know you're not supposed to open your door at night but I couldn't sleep, thinking about him.

SALLY   Well, I wouldn't lose any more sleep: I saw him first thing and he was right enough.

PATIENCE   Was he?

SALLY   Singing away to himself.

PATIENCE   Oh, that's good. It's just... I know he wouldn't do anything but sometimes, when he comes at night – now the nights are drawing in –

SALLY   You did the right thing.

PATIENCE   Mmm...

SALLY   You're right about the nights drawing in, though. It'll be Christmas before we know it.

PATIENCE   Oh, don't say that, the hunt hasn't started.

SALLY   They've been out cubbing.

PATIENCE   Oh, yes, there was all that business with the greenhouse at the Rectory.

SALLY   Caroline told me.

PATIENCE   She's very up on things is Caroline; very on the ball. She's certainly shaken us up at the WI. We had a speaker in about that refugee camp. Only a young woman: French but her English was marvellous. *Medicins Sans Frontieres.* Like *Jeux Sans Frontieres* – do you remember that? Not like that really, but you know what I mean: French.

SALLY   Wasn't that Prince Edward?

PATIENCE   What?

SALLY   *It's a Knock Out?*

PATIENCE *(beat)* Stuart Hall. *(Pause) You* should come to the WI.

SALLY   I've barely time to get to church these days.

PATIENCE   You do too much.

SALLY   Keith's working all hours but if it wasn't for what I bring in...

Pause.

PATIENCE   How's his dad?

SALLY *(beat)* He just sits there. *(Beat)* It's like he's given up.

PATIENCE   They were always a very close couple, him and Pat. You'd see them sometimes... I said to Leslie once: I said, 'Why don't you look at me like that?' But he just looked at me. But not like that.

SALLY   But when Leslie died, you didn't...

PATIENCE *(beat)* I think it's worse for fellas. I don't think they know what to do.

SALLY   If the kids were a bit older it wouldn't be so bad; you know, they could help more, but as it is...

PATIENCE   And they all want feeding.

SALLY   Tell me!

PATIENCE   It's as well you've no more.

SALLY   It is.

PATIENCE   And what's happened over that business with your lambs. Have they caught anyone?

SALLY   I can't see they ever will.

PATIENCE   It's still going on?

SALLY   Another two last week. We've not told the kids; don't want them upset.

PATIENCE   I mean who'd do something like that?

SALLY   You'd wonder, wouldn't you?

PATIENCE   You would.

SALLY   Right. That's you done. Do you want some of your spray on it?

PATIENCE I'd better. Yes. *(Sally sprays Patience's hair)* Lovely. *(Pause)* I've left your money on the side. Will you have a toffee?

SALLY No, thanks. *(Beat)* Oh, you've given me too much.

PATIENCE No.

SALLY I'll get you some change.

PATIENCE I don't want any change.

SALLY But –

PATIENCE Take it. *(Pause)* Take it.

SALLY *(putting money in her bag)* I'll give you that special shampoo next time.

PATIENCE That's right.

They go.

John runs on and looks behind him. He hides.

CAROLINE David bloody Haworth. People are so... deferential you'd think the sun shone out of his... And he's so infuriatingly polite. If he got off his high horse once in a while... But of course he wouldn't do that because he looks so good on it. *(Beat)* That's what he thinks, obviously. *(Beat)* How anyone could hunt such a beautiful creature is totally beyond me. It's barbaric.

John comes out and proffers a dead rabbit...

Sally enters with cake making paraphernalia...

SALLY And what did you say?

CAROLINE Thanks but no thanks!

John runs off...

SALLY You should've had it. Rabbit stew: lovely!

CAROLINE I think that's taking local food a bit too literally. And where would he have got it from?

SALLY Road-kill probably.

CAROLINE Will he eat it?

SALLY Dunno

CAROLINE Well, at least it'll have died for a purpose.

SALLY Unlike the poor –

CAROLINE It's true. *(Beat)* Why they don't just say they enjoy it, I don't know. But no, it's all: 'The fox is a pest –

SALLY Which it is.

CAROLINE – and the hunt is an effective means of pest control.' And the next minute they're saying they hardly ever kill anything –

SALLY Which with this lot round here is probably about it. I should think Keith shoots more foxes than the hunt ever gets. But if they want to ride round all day chasing the damn things, where's the harm in that?

CAROLINE The harm in that, Sally, is that it's inhumane.

SALLY Look, in the countryside we treat death... A cow has a dead calf; a calf dies – sometimes a cow dies; sheep are always dying. They die for no reason. You want something to die: you buy some sheep. So death doesn't have the same... We've got different attitudes.

CAROLINE That's saying you agree with it.

SALLY I'm not bothered one way or the other.

CAROLINE I just don't think hunting a defenceless animal is much of an advert for a civilised society.

SALLY So you've said! *(Beat)* You're worrying about the wrong things, that's all I'm saying. There are people dying in stupid bloody wars all over the place. Worry about that.

CAROLINE I do. And I wonder if one thing doesn't lead to the other.

SALLY   You've lost me now.

CAROLINE Violence begets violence.

SALLY   Don't be daft.

Pause.

CAROLINE You don't even hunt.

SALLY   I don't even ride!

CAROLINE And yet you'll defend people who do it.

SALLY   I'll defend their right to do it, yes. It's part of how things are: the way we do things in the country.

CAROLINE 'Country ways'.

SALLY   If you like.

CAROLINE *(Beat)* If it was a working class pursuit like dog racing or darts or something, the police'd be down on it like a ton of bricks. But because it's moneyed people –

SALLY   It's not only moneyed people.

CAROLINE You can't be poor and keep a horse.

SALLY   You can work yourself half to death to do it. People do.

CAROLINE Why?

SALLY   Because it matters to them. Because it's all they're interested in. Because they love it.

CAROLINE *(beat)* Up from London half of them.

SALLY   So?

CAROLINE So they're hardly the genuine article.

SALLY *(beat)* People just don't like being told how to live their lives.

CAROLINE I'm not...

SALLY   But you are.

Pause.

CAROLINE David Haworth: the great 'I am'.

SALLY That's not David.

CAROLINE He behaves like he is.

SALLY He's just another farmer like the rest of us.

CAROLINE Hardly!

SALLY Methinks the lady doth protest too much.

CAROLINE What? *(Beat)* The lady, for your information, is happily married and doesn't protest at all.

SALLY If you say so.

CAROLINE Sally!

SALLY Mm?

CAROLINE I'd no idea you were such a stirrer!

SALLY Who me? *(Beat)* Still, he's a good looking fella.

CAROLINE Well...

SALLY Ah!

CAROLINE He could be as good looking as you like, I could never find a man who hunts attractive. To say nothing of the way he farms.

SALLY Oh, don't get onto that!

CAROLINE There's no need for all this spraying –

SALLY Please? *(Pause)* Piece of cake?

CAROLINE Er...

SALLY It's not been sprayed or anything.

CAROLINE Ha, bloody ha!

SALLY Well, don't if you don't want.

CAROLINE No, I do want.

SALLY *(cutting cake)* I can't stop eating at the moment.

CAROLINE *(beat)* You don't think..?

SALLY *(beat)* Don't be daft. I can't remember the last time me and Keith... although there was that morning –

CAROLINE I rest my case!

SALLY Well, you can pick it up again: you're on the wrong track.

Pause.

CAROLINE Would you like another one?

SALLY Two's plenty, thank you very much. *(Beat)* Now give me a hand with this...

They go.

DAVID We've heard from Chris... on their way any day now. A soldier goes wherever he's sent – that's the deal – and when you're in there yourself you don't really think about it – try not to – but when it's your son... And Mary's... *(Beat)* Still, if he comes out of it with nothing worse than I did he won't be doing so bad. *(Beat)* As long as he gets home.

He goes.

Sally with a pregnancy testing kit.

SALLY Replace cap... Windows facing up... Positive results may be observed in one minute or less depending on the level of hCG. *(Beat)* Right...

John is singing somewhere.

JOHN *(sings)* I am a brisk and bonny lass
and free from care and strife
And sweetly as the hours pass I love a country life.
At wake or fair I'm always there where pleasure's to be seen
Though poor I am contented: I'm as happy as a queen.

SALLY   Thank you, John! Oh, come on...

JOHN *(sings)* In summer or in winter we never ought to grieve
For in the time of hardship each neighbour should relieve.
But still I think of a country life while others do surpass
So sit me down contented: I'm a happy country lass.

SALLY   Right... *(She looks at the test.)*
Oh, God. *(Beat)* Oh, my God.

A gust of wind. Sally shivers.

John looks up at the sky.

Night falls.

PART THREE: WINTER

Darkness

JOHN   And lo, the angel of the Lord said unto them: fear not; for behold I bring you tidings of great joy!

Light.

All sing:

ALL *(sing)* Shepherds arise, be not afraid
            With hasty steps repair to David's city:
            Sing honour to our blest infant there
            To our blest infant there

            Sing, sing on earth;
            Sing, sing on earth eternal praises sing
            To our redeemer, to our redeemer
            And our heavenly king

            For our saviour came on earth
            For us his life he gave
            To save us from eternal death
            And to raise us from the grave

John runs off...

PATIENCE   Talk about peace on earth and goodwill to all men. The things you read about; see on TV... The other night, I thought, 'Why doesn't somebody do something?' And then I thought if everyone's thinking this, who's this somebody going to be? I know it sounds a bit puffed up. Leslie would turn in his grave – not that he's in a grave: he's scattered on the roses at the crematorium – but he wouldn't like it if he knew what I've done cos he didn't hold with people making a fuss but you can't just sit back and do nothing, can you, puffed up or not?

SALLY   Bernard's no better. I don't think anyone realised how much he relied on Pat and since she's gone... Things weigh on his mind. When *he* took the farm over from *his* dad it was thriving: employed eight men. Now... And none of the politicians seem interested. You wonder why people want to be politicians. Maybe they go into it with good intentions but they all seem to end up the same. It's all votes, isn't it? And there are so few of us left anymore we don't count.

DAVID   The 'antis' don't know what they're talking about. Most farmers will go to the masters and say, 'Hunt on my land because I've been having trouble.' And then the hunt takes their fallen stock. It's a real and passionate community, one of the few continuous threads in a time of change. People want to hold onto it. In Bicester on Boxing Day there'll be thousands out. And it's not just those who ride: there's farriers; B&B's; livery stables. I'm not saying there aren't some people who are genuinely upset by it but you have to look the other way, don't you?

CAROLINE God knows I don't want to make enemies but there was a vote in parliament; there was a law passed. You wouldn't think so. 'But it's traditional, been going on for centuries.' You could say the same about... bear-baiting, slavery... But fox hunting... 'People rely on it for their livelihoods.' I don't remember the Countryside Alliance making a fuss when they closed the pits. People relied on mining.

PATIENCE You see I've written a letter, to the Prime Minister. I said, 'All these things going on: people aren't listening to each other. We've got to listen. We've got to get past what "I" want and "you" want and find out what's best for "us". We don't have to agree but we have to listen or we'll never understand and then where do we go?' *(Beat)* I sit by the school sometimes – there's a bench – watch the children playing, and I think: what sort of world have we made for you? Is it a better one than we found? And it doesn't seem to me that it is.

SALLY   The days of the small family farm have gone. But that's not how Bernard sees it. He sees how hard it is for Keith, for all of us, and I think he blames himself. *(Beat)* They say things go in cycles but I don't think it'll ever come back. It'd take another war to make farming important again and nobody wants that.

DAVID   No word from Chris. Not since just after they got there. If they've gone into the mountains – which is where he thought they were headed – they must be up to their necks. It's pretty bloody terrain by all accounts. We watch the news, of course, keep our eyes on the papers... But we don't really talk about it. Probably just as well. I mean, after all, what's to say?

CAROLINE   And what really gets me is they think they can just carry on regardless. They write letters to *The Telegraph* about kids in hooded tops but when it's them, suddenly it's OK to break the law. Matt says I should keep out of it and I know it doesn't concern him the same way but then he's hardly ever here. I'm lucky if he stays one night these days. Still he's home for the holidays.

Caroline helps Patience home with her shopping...

PATIENCE   Home again, home again, jiggety-jig. *(Beat)* Oh, no, it's jiggety-jog isn't it?

CAROLINE   Is it?

PATIENCE   To market, to market to buy a fat... Anyhow, jig or jog, he'll be home and so are we. *(Examining her purchase)* Sales are not what they were, are they? Still, I needed some new pants. Will you have a cuppa?

CAROLINE   No thanks.

PATIENCE   I expect you're busy.

CAROLINE   No. *(Pause)* Have you read the latest Newsletter?

PATIENCE   No. No, I haven't had a chance.

CAROLINE I'm trying to get a debate going. About pesticides, spraying.

PATIENCE Farmers have always sprayed.

CAROLINE That's just it, they haven't.

PATIENCE Well, they've sprayed as long as I can remember. Leslie: that was one of his regular jobs with the tractor, spraying for David's father.

CAROLINE I didn't know he worked for the estate.

PATIENCE All his life. Never did him any harm.

CAROLINE *(beat)* What did he die of – if you don't mind my asking?

PATIENCE Cancer.

CAROLINE Patience, cancers are one of the very things linked to the use of agro-chemicals.

PATIENCE *(beat)* I don't think you should say –

CAROLINE I'm not saying in Leslie's case but –

PATIENCE They wouldn't let people use them if that was true. I mean, the government and that, they'd tell people. They have advisers, the politicians, you know: experts.

CAROLINE And what if these expert advisers were paid by the people who make the chemicals?

PATIENCE Well, they wouldn't be, would they?

CAROLINE But they are.

PATIENCE *(beat)* No!

CAROLINE Yes. *(Pause)* And it's all for profit.

PATIENCE David's not.

CAROLINE Isn't he? He owns half the village.

PATIENCE Not these days.

CAROLINE No, because he's sold it off.

PATIENCE   You can't have it both ways, Caroline.

CAROLINE   I bet he owns this place.

PATIENCE   Well...

CAROLINE   And how much rent does he charge you? I'm sorry – that's none of my business. I'm sorry. I just get so –

PATIENCE   He doesn't.

CAROLINE   What?

PATIENCE   He doesn't charge me anything. I mean I pay the water and electric and... But no, since Leslie died, he's let me have it. Good of him, isn't it?

CAROLINE *(beat)* Yes. Yes, it is. *(Pause)* But he's still part of the whole... I mean the very fact that he hunts.

PATIENCE   He's the Master.

CAROLINE   And don't we know it. But there was a law passed.

PATIENCE   I don't think David would break the law. He's a County Councillor.

CAROLINE   A Tory County Councillor.

PATIENCE   I've always voted for him. He was in the Falklands; he was decorated.

CAROLINE   I'm sorry, I don't see –

PATIENCE   I'm just saying. *(Beat)* He was wounded.

CAROLINE   Was he? *(Beat)* Anyway, have you seen Sally?

PATIENCE *(beat)* Yes, she did my hair Thursday. She's very good, you know. You should have yours done. *(Beat)* She's not showing yet.

CAROLINE   No.

PATIENCE   I think it's going to be hard for her with another one.

CAROLINE *(beat)* Yes.

PATIENCE She never says but I think things are a bit of a struggle.

CAROLINE With the farm?

PATIENCE And Bernard. Can't be easy.

CAROLINE At least she's got a husband to call her own. *(Beat)* I'm sorry, I didn't mean to say that.

Pause.

PATIENCE You want to talk about it?

CAROLINE No. *(Beat)* Yes.

Pause.

PATIENCE Is he playing away, do you think?

CAROLINE I don't know.

PATIENCE My Leslie did it once. I'm not sure how much went on but that's not the point, is it? They go away from you. I mean they're in the room, at the table... in the bed with you but they're not there. He was... It was after... I lost a baby.

CAROLINE Oh, I'm sorry.

PATIENCE It was a long while ago now! Sixty years nearly. But you never forget... Anyway, for a long while after, I didn't want... you know. And fellers have needs, don't they? *(Beat)* It didn't last. He came back. He hadn't really been anywhere but he came back. So fingers crossed, eh?

CAROLINE *(beat)* Did you never have any more children?

PATIENCE No. They took it all away. They did that then.

Pause. Patience looks at the newsletter...

PATIENCE Oh!

CAROLINE What?

PATIENCE I don't think you meant to say this.

CAROLINE What?

Patience hands her the newsletter...

PATIENCE The caption to the photo...

CAROLINE *(reading)* Longton Estate owner, David Haworth looks understandably out of breath after his two-hour sponsored w... *(Beat)* Oh, my God! *(Beat)* It was supposed to say 'walk'.

PATIENCE What a difference one letter can make!

CAROLINE That's terrible.

PATIENCE People might not notice.

CAROLINE You did.

PATIENCE Well... Have you delivered them yet?

CAROLINE Only to every house in the village.

PATIENCE These things happen.

CAROLINE As if I'm not unpopular enough as it is.

PATIENCE It always takes a while for people to get used to new faces. When I first came here some were very off-hand. Coming from Birmingham they thought I was a foreigner and then I went and married the best looking chap in the village – that put a few noses out, I can tell you!

CAROLINE How long before things settled down?

PATIENCE Oh, about forty years. *(Perhaps they laugh)* Toffee?

CAROLINE Thanks.

Sally in the farmyard...

SALLY We've been wondering what to do. What with they way things are and the baby coming and... Keith's going to try and get a bit more contract work but I look at him sometimes when he's asleep and he looks worn out; like an old man. He's forty-two. And Carl's after the latest England kit for his birthday – cheap imitations not acceptable – and Lucy wants to go on the school trip and we've still not had all our Single Farm Payment so we've had to borrow some more and now the bank's making noises, loud ones, and it's me who deals with it. *(Beat)* And another two sheep this month. That's fourteen in all. Madness.

John is there...

JOHN	Behold! A virgin shall conceive.
SALLY	Bit late for that.
JOHN	And she shall call his name Emanuel.
SALLY	I don't think so. *(Beat)* Don't even know if it's a boy.
JOHN	Can you feel it inside you?
SALLY	Not yet.
JOHN	Can I?
SALLY	No.
JOHN	I'll be gentle.
SALLY	No!

JOHN *(proffering a rabbit skin)* I brought a present!

SALLY	Oh.
JOHN	To wrap the Baby Bunting in.

Pause. The sound of dogs. John freezes.

SALLY It's all right –

DAVID *(off)* Hello there!

John runs away.

SALLY John!

DAVID *(entering)* Was that –?

SALLY Yes. You know what's he's like. *(Putting down her load)* Anyhow...

DAVID   Should you be doing that?

SALLY *(beat)* Oh, no, it's fine. I'm fine.

DAVID   Keith not about?

SALLY   He's taken Bernard to the doctor's.

DAVID   Not flu, is it?

SALLY   No, he's just... you know... Pat... missing Pat... how things are here. He just sits there.

DAVID   Sad to see it happen.

SALLY   So we thought the doctor might... Anyway!

DAVID   And the children?

SALLY   Oh, they're fine. Growing! What about your Christopher? Any news?

DAVID   No. We don't expect any. Not for a while. But as far as we know...

SALLY   Yes.

DAVID   But I'm sure you didn't ask me over to chat about our respective offspring.

SALLY   No. Well, yes in a way.

DAVID   Oh?

SALLY *(beat)* With the baby coming... I'll have to cut back on my hairdressing and cake making for a while...

DAVID   Have you had your Single Farm Payment?

SALLY   Most of it... But on a farm this size...

DAVID   Sometimes I wonder why any of us do it at all.

SALLY   I say that to Keith sometimes but he says, What else would we do? Anyway, we've been thinking – taking a leaf out of your book, really.

DAVID   Diversification?

SALLY   I was reading about paint-balling.

DAVID   Oh yes.

SALLY   You know, fellas chasing each other about...

DAVID   Yes.

SALLY   It's very popular apparently.

DAVID   It's a good thought but Ben Roberts over at Kingston's just started it.

SALLY   Oh.

DAVID   Great minds.

SALLY   Yes. Or there's the old barn.

DAVID   Conversion?

SALLY   I wondered, with your being on the council...

DAVID   I'm not on the planning committee.

SALLY   No, I didn't mean... I just wondered... if you thought it was worth putting in an application.

DAVID   You'd have objections from the conservation brigade.

SALLY   But –

DAVID   I absolutely agree with you. This is our livelihood we're talking about – that's what these people don't understand. It's like hunting or crop protection. I've had Caroline Bishop on the phone every five minutes.

SALLY   I know she's got very strong views.

DAVID   That's as maybe but she's very little idea of the realities of country life. *(Beat)* And did I hear you'd lost some more sheep?

SALLY   Two.

DAVID   This is ridiculous! Still no word from the police?

SALLY   I don't think it's very high on their agenda.

DAVID   Bring back the village bobby, that's what I say.

SALLY So if you want to tell Kenny, he can come and pick up the carcasses for the hounds.

DAVID Thanks. *(Beat)* Sorry I couldn't be more...

SALLY No, that's all right. I'll think of something.

DAVID Keith's a very lucky man.

SALLY That's what I tell him. *(Beat)* Well... Better get on.

DAVID Absolutely. Don't let the bastards grind you down, eh?

SALLY No. No, that's right...

David goes.

Sally feels the baby move. She goes.

The sound of a WWI bombardment fading away...

JOHN Dear Mum,

I know you were cross with me when I went away as I had lied to you about my joining up and lied to the recruiting sergeant about my age. But I am writing this letter as I would not wish you to be cross with me no more.

You might have heard that Petey died but not, I think, how it went or that I was with him when it happened. Since we came here to France, things have been hard and you would not credit the noise the big guns can make nor the mud and muck there is here. You know how the long meadow can be, when it has been raining for a week and the cows have churned it up down by the river – well that is not to be compared. And rats! I swear I never saw so many nor so big. Old Sam Elkins would have a field day with his gun.

Anyhow, last week we was going forward after a long period of holding our position and the bombardment was terrible but I was with Petey as ever I was and one minute he was talking – yes, and swearing: you know Petey – and the next, the shell exploded and he was blown clean in the air. And when I called he did not answer. So I pulled him towards me and then I saw that he could neither see nor hear me as his face was quite gone and all the insides of his head was there. And I could not look at him – my oldest friend since we was boys – and all I knew was that I must get away. And so I ran and hid myself as best I could, like a fox gone to ground, and whimpering all the while like a baby.

And that is where they found me, whimpering still and in my own mess. And yesterday I was tried by the Court Martial and tomorrow I am to be shot. And you'd think I would be frightened - because they tell me I am a coward and maybe I am – but in truth I am not afraid and am only glad that I will no more have to see the picture in my head of poor Petey without his face.

I know you shall never see this letter as you can no more read than I can write but I can write well enough in my head so forgive me, mother, for the lie I told you and for leaving you when there was all the ploughing to be done.

Your loving son,

John.

The sound of a firing squad...

PATIENCE   It was in the paper today: 'Captain Christopher Haworth, twenty-nine, of the 2ⁿᵈ Battalion, Royal Warwickshire Regiment.' Captain! I remember him as a little boy – cheeky smile, always up to something, a proper lad *(And she remembers her own son)*. It'll be hard for David. And his wife. They say she drinks. And who could blame her now? He did look handsome in his uniform.

John in the spinney. David enters with a bottle...

DAVID   Chris..? Chris is that – *(John turns round.)* Oh. *(Drinks)* I've been drinking. Obviously. But why not, eh? Why not? *(Drinks)* Stray bullet. They think it might have been one of ours. Ironic really. Is ironic the right word? Do I mean ironic? Or do I mean stupid? Bloody stupid and pointless and... They sent a chaplain round to talk to us. Mary wouldn't see him. Still... We're going to bury him here. They're sending the body back to us: the remains. Apparently it would have been pretty instantaneous. So that's a comfort. *(Drinks)* Help me. Help me, please.

John holds David in his arms. David weeps.

David runs off.

JOHN   And God shall wipe away all the tears
from their eyes;
And there shall be no more death, neither sorrow
nor crying,
Neither shall there be any more pain.
Weeping may endure for a night
But joy cometh in the morning.

In church.

ALL *(sing)* Abide with me. Fast falls the eventide.
The darkness deepens, Lord with me abide.
When other helpers fail and comforts flee,
Help of the helpless, abide with me.

DAVID   This is the saddest duty any father can perform. The saddest and the hardest but in Chris's case – my son's case – also the proudest. Chris was a fine young man and a fine soldier and he died doing his duty and that is a fine thing to be able to say however hard it is for his family to bear his loss. In many ways Chris was more than my son: he was, in a very real sense, my friend and my soulmate. We shared many things: a love of this place, of the land and the village – and I know that many of you who saw him grow up here were hugely fond of him in your turn. We shared also our love of professional soldiering and above all, perhaps, we shared a love of hunting... and I will, I think, never again mount a horse or call a hound to heel without Chris being with me. *(Pause)* He would have been touched that so many of you have taken the time to remember him and on his behalf, and that of my wife, I would like to thank you all for being here today. *(Pause)* To conclude, here is a poem Chris must have cared for or at any rate one he copied out because I found it yesterday when I was looking through his old school books.

He reads...

> He could not die when trees were green
> For he loved the time too well.
> I am: yet what I am none cares or knows.
> I long for scenes where man has never trod
> A place where woman never smiled or wept
> There to abide with my creator, God
> And sleep as I in childhood sweetly slept
> Untroubling and untroubled where I lie
> The grass below – above the vaulted sky.

ALL *(sing)* When other helpers fail and comforts flee,
Help of the helpless, abide with me.

In the churchyard after the funeral.

PATIENCE   It was a lovely service.

DAVID   Was it?

PATIENCE   Didn't you think so?

DAVID   I don't know what to think anymore. I just keep thinking about the last time he was home – how full of hope he was, how full of life. You've no idea, Patience... to lose your child...

PATIENCE   No. I'm not sure anyone can understand that. Except God perhaps. I think He might understand.

DAVID   What kind of God is it that takes a young man, a mother's son..?

PATIENCE   Or gives his own.

DAVID   What?

PATIENCE   We mustn't turn away from Him. That's what Leslie used to say.

DAVID   I don't know where He is, Patience.

PATIENCE   I know. He can be hard to find sometimes.

DAVID   I'm not even sure I believe any more.

PATIENCE   No, I don't know if I believe exactly. But I think I belong. And that's a comfort.

DAVID   Comfort...

PATIENCE *(after a moment)* You should go home now.

DAVID   Yes.

PATIENCE   Your wife will be wondering where you are.

DAVID   I'll just walk up to Higham Wood.

PATIENCE *(after a moment)* I'll say a prayer.

DAVID   Who for?

PATIENCE   For all of us.

She watches him go.

John runs on and looks at the sky.

PATIENCE   What is it, John?

He looks at Patience.

PATIENCE   What?

Night falls.

PART FOUR: SPRING

Darkness.

JOHN   Rise up, my love, my fair one and come away.
For lo, the winter is past, the rain is over and gone;
the flowers appear on the earth; the time of the
singing birds is come; and the voice of the turtle is
heard in our land.

Light.

ALL *(sing)* The echoin' horn sounds well in the morn
To call the brave sportsmen away
When the cry of the hounds makes a musical sound
So greatly enlightens the day, the day
So greatly enlightens the day.
We will away to some joys, to hear some
brave noise
Our hounds they will open their throats
When the fox he breaks cover, hark forward,
high over
We will follow their musical notes, their notes
We will follow their musical notes.
Over mountains he flies then afterwards dies,
He has led us an excellent chase
We will take off his brush then home we will rush
In order our spirits to raise, to raise
In order our spirits to raise.
With a bottle and friend an evening we'll spend
We'll crown the brave sports of the day
And our wives shall at night give us great delight
And so drive all our sorrows away, away
And so drive all our sorrows away.

John runs off...

PATIENCE   When I was little – when I was a little girl, I
used to play a game, sort of hide and seek, and my dad'd say
– he was a bit of a comedian, my dad – he'd say, 'Oh, where's

my Patience? My Patience has run out!' And then he'd come and find me – cos I'd only be under the table or summat daft. *(Pause)* Well, now my patience has run out. Cos he never answered. You know, the Prime Minister. No.

And then the other day I open the paper and there's an article about that young chap as was shot on the underground the other year, about his parents, how they still can't understand how it happened. Or why.

And no one can explain to them. Well, what could they say? 'We were all so frightened we never stopped to ask questions and so we shot him? We killed him, your son: here's his body.' And that's when I had my big idea: to go to London and make a stink.

SALLY   I'm going to have to think about doing less soon and then when the baby comes... Keith's working all hours – late lambing - but the bank never gives up. They're worse than the kids and Bernard... The doctor's had him on anti-depressants but I can't see it's helped much. *(Beat)* But I've had an idea. *(Beat)* It could make all the difference. *(Beat)* So fingers crossed, eh?

DAVID   'Blessed is the man who expects nothing: for he shall never be disappointed.' My father was fond of that one. And you have to try and keep things in perspective. Mary... Well, obviously. It's easier for me, with the estate; things to do but no point letting everything... They've won then, haven't they? They've bloody won.

CAROLINE   There's been a planning application. No prizes for guessing who's behind it. Nine 'Executive-style homes.' I bet. Faux Tudor monstrosities more like. And where does he want to build them? Longton Spinney – practically the last bit of real bio-diversity for miles. Matt says I should keep out. What's it got to do with me? And I say everything because I live here, this is my home and I can't just stand back and let some developer sweep in and... *(Beat)* So I'm lodging an objection. This village is beautiful. We have to guard that.

PATIENCE   I've still got Leslie's gun, you see. Not that it was his really: he took it off a German at the end of the war; bullets too. So it's not new but he always kept it beautiful: used to clean it with an oily rag; frightened me to death. Then, after he died, I didn't know what to do with it. I was hoping they'd have one of them amnesties, you know, where you can pop along to the police station on the QT, no questions asked. They had one for knives but I haven't got a knife – in fact I could do with one – my bread knife's US, but they never had one for guns so I've still got it. It's in the wardrobe, all wrapped up in a Tupperware.

John runs by, pursued, and hides.

David working at the estate. Caroline enters.

CAROLINE   David.

DAVID   Caroline.

Pause. There is nothing to be said of other things.

CAROLINE   Did you get my email?

DAVID   Which one? There have been so many.

CAROLINE *(beat)* About the spinney.

DAVID   Oh, the plans for the new houses.

CAROLINE   'Executive Style Homes.'

DAVID   A small development of six detached properties plus some much needed affordable housing provision.

CAROLINE   I can see why you're a politician, David.

DAVID   I'll take that as a compliment.

CAROLINE   Take it any way you like.

Pause.

DAVID   The village desperately needs some affordable housing.

CAROLINE Since your lot sold off all the council houses...

DAVID I voted against that one.

CAROLINE ...and the local estate sold off its tied cottages.

DAVID Modern, mechanised farming simply doesn't require the man-power of the post-war years.

CAROLINE How convenient.

DAVID You think it was a matter of choice?

CAROLINE Wasn't it?

DAVID If the estate hadn't rationalised, it would have gone to the wall long since and we wouldn't be employing anyone.

CAROLINE Or enjoying such healthy profits.

DAVID You'll have to forgive me for making a living and providing jobs for the local community.

CAROLINE You'll have your violin out next about all the jobs that depend on hunting.

DAVID I'd say that was beyond dispute.

CAROLINE Really? Well, if it were up to me –

DAVID Which fortunately it isn't, or what pleasures would remain?

CAROLINE It's not a question of pleasures.

DAVID No?

CAROLINE It's a question of what sort of world we want to live in.

DAVID Well I'd like to live in one where people are allowed to get on with their lives.

CAROLINE So no rules of any kind?

DAVID The fewer the better.

CAROLINE Yes, I can see that would suit you perfectly.

And I'm sure you feel the same about crop spraying.

DAVID　Heavens, Caroline, you certainly cover the ground, don't you?

CAROLINE　The land is our common heritage. Yet farmers seem to think they can do whatever they like with it – tearing out hedges –

DAVID　No one's taking out hedges these days.

CAROLINE　Only because they're paying you to put them back. And it's the same with chemicals. To say nothing of the dangers involved.

DAVID　All my workers, if and when they're using chemicals, wear protective masks and clothing.

CAROLINE　Yes, but the rest of us don't.

DAVID　There's no evidence that crop protection affects the health of either local people or consumers.

CAROLINE　There was no evidence about asbestos for years. The truth is, we simply don't know. It's sheer arrogance.

DAVID　It's market pressure. People want cheap food.

CAROLINE　I don't. I'm prepared to pay a premium for naturally grown, local produce.

DAVID　Well, bully for you. Gold star! Green goddess!

Pause.

DAVID　I'm sorry... That was rude of me.

CAROLINE　No. *(Beat)* I can afford it, you're right.

Pause.

DAVID　We seem rather to have strayed from the original point of your visit.

CAROLINE　Yes. I simply wanted you to know that I've lodged an objection to the planning application. I'm not saying I'm opposed to any additional housing in the village – especially affordable housing , but Longton Spinney is not the place for it to happen and I think it's irresponsible of you to think of destroying it.

DAVID   Caroline, Longton Spinney isn't part of the estate.

CAROLINE What?

DAVID   I don't own Longton Spinney.

CAROLINE Then who does?

DAVID   The Armstrongs.

CAROLINE Sally and Keith?

DAVID   Bernard's father won it from my old dad in a wager. Before the war. Wasn't worth much at the time. *(Beat)* Is there anything else?

CAROLINE No... No.

Perhaps John runs on and hides again.

PATIENCE   I've been to Banbury, bought my train ticket. I didn't ask Caroline. I got the bus. And who should I meet at the station but Mrs Parker – Mrs Nosy Parker, Leslie used to call her. 'Oh, Mrs Dodds... London? Do you think you'll be all right with all the terrorism?' 'Oh, London doesn't worry me. I'm from Birmingham originally.' 'Are you really? I always thought you were a villager.' 'That's how much you know.' I didn't say that, I just thought it. 'Oh, it's nice to be mistaken for a local after all this time.' Mrs Nosy Parker. *(Beat)* And I bought myself a decent bread knife. £5.99. I didn't think that was bad.

She unpacks her purchases. John enters.

JOHN   Out of the depths have I cried to thee, O lord!
Lord, hear my voice: let thine ears be attentive to
the voice of my supplication.

PATIENCE   Oh, John... I didn't see you there. You made me jump!

JOHN   I was a voice crying in the wilderness.

PATIENCE   You certainly were.

JOHN   But you heard me, you who have ears to hear.

PATIENCE   I should think half the village heard you, ears or not.

JOHN   I was a stranger in a strange land.

PATIENCE   Well, do you want some cold toast? There's jam with it. Mrs Fraser's not mine, so you're quite safe. Or if you wait, you can have some soup. It's only out of a tin but it's Baxters: leek and potato.

JOHN   I was hungry and ye gave me meat; I was thirsty and ye gave me drink; I was a stranger and you took me in.

PATIENCE   Yes, well, I don't mind taking you in when it's light. It's when you come at night that I don't like opening the door.

JOHN   Knock, knock.

PATIENCE   Who's there?

JOHN   John.

PATIENCE   That's right.

JOHN   The foxes have holes and the birds of the air have nests but the Son of Man hath not where to lay his head. *(Beat)* You won't let them take me?

PATIENCE   Who's that then?

JOHN   Magistrate's men.

PATIENCE   Oh, you don't want to worry about them.

JOHN   They hunt me like an animal.

PATIENCE   They're long gone.

JOHN   They've man traps.

PATIENCE   No.

JOHN   The dogs will find me out.

PATIENCE   Don't get yourself worked up.

JOHN   They ask no questions.

PATIENCE   John –

JOHN   They would shoot me and I do none harm.

PATIENCE   You're getting all upset. There's no-one's going to shoot you.

JOHN   No?

PATIENCE   There's no one coming.

JOHN   Promise?

PATIENCE   Promise. *(Pause)* Shall I get that soup?

The sound of dogs, off-stage.

JOHN   What's that?

PATIENCE   Oh, that'll just be David, coming to check up.

JOHN   You lied to me.

PATIENCE   No.

JOHN *(seizing the knife)* You lied!

PATIENCE   Now, John, don't be silly.

DAVID *(off)* Hello, there, Patience.

John panics and seizes Patience, holding the knife to her throat.

David enters.

DAVID   I've just come – What the hell's going on?

PATIENCE   It's all right, David

DAVID   Put that knife down, John.

PATIENCE   He's all upset.

DAVID   Put it down, I said.

John hesitates, releases Patience but doesn't know what to do next.

DAVID   Now put that knife down or I'm calling the police.

John edges to the door.

DAVID   John, if you don't put that knife down this minute, I'm going to come over there and take it off you.

John hesitates, drops the knife, and runs out.

PATIENCE   Oh, my word, what a drama!

DAVID *(retrieving the knife)* Are you all right?

PATIENCE   Oh, I'm fine. He didn't hurt me.

DAVID *(taking out mobile)* I'd better ring –

PATIENCE   Oh, David, don't do that.

DAVID   Patience!

PATIENCE   Well, what would the police do?

DAVID   Lock him up if they've any sense.

PATIENCE   He wouldn't harm anyone.

DAVID   He had a knife.

PATIENCE   It was just my new bread knife.

DAVID   Yes, and he was holding it to your throat.

PATIENCE   He didn't mean... He was frightened. He heard the dogs and... I don't think he'd've done anything.

DAVID *(dialling)* We can't take that risk.

PATIENCE   Please, I'd rather you didn't. *(Beat)* We all go a bit mad sometimes, don't we? *(Beat)* Let's leave it?

DAVID *(cancelling the call)* He should be put away.

PATIENCE   David, don't be like that.

DAVID   Like what? When I think –

PATIENCE   I know. *(Pause)* How are things?

DAVID   …

PATIENCE   How's your wife?

DAVID   …

PATIENCE   Tell her I was asking after her.

DAVID   Yes.

PATIENCE *(pause)* I was going to make some soup, will you have some?

DAVID   I won't, if you'll forgive me.

PATIENCE   It's Baxters.

DAVID   Even so. I'd better get back.

PATIENCE   Yes.

DAVID   Now, you're sure you're all right?

PATIENCE   As rain.

DAVID   And you won't let me call the police?

PATIENCE   No. Thank you, no.

DAVID   Well, promise me you will if he comes back.

PATIENCE   Cross my heart.

 DAVID   Right. *(Going but then remembering)* Oh, it's the last meet of the season, Saturday. I know you like to see us off.

PATIENCE   Saturday?

DAVID   The Eleventh. Should be quite a turn out.

PATIENCE *(beat)* Oh, I shan't be able to make it this year. There's something I have to do.

DAVID   Not to worry. *(Beat)* There's always next year.

PATIENCE *(beat)* Yes, that's right. There is, isn't there?

John looking for somewhere to hide.

Sally in the famyard mixing sheep dip. She is now visably pregnant. Caroline enters.

CAROLINE We need to talk.

SALLY Do we?

CAROLINE All right, I need to talk; to explain.

Pause.

SALLY Go on then.

CAROLINE Longton Spinney... I'd no idea... When I lodged the objection, I'd no idea it belonged to you.

SALLY And would that've made a difference?

CAROLINE I thought it was part of the estate.

SALLY And now you know it isn't, does that make a difference?

CAROLINE *(beat)* It's not just any piece of woodland, you know.

SALLY Is that right?

CAROLINE The wildflowers there –

SALLY Hart's Tongue, Stitchwort, Sagewood. I know.

CAROLINE Then –

SALLY Why are you doing this?

CAROLINE It's nothing personal, you know that.

SALLY Feels pretty personal to me.

CAROLINE I mean it's a matter of principle.

SALLY To you, maybe. Maybe to you it's a matter of principle. To us it's a matter of survival. We need to sell that land. We need the money it's going to bring in. Not want, not 'it would be quite nice so I can have the guest toilet redecorated' – need.

CAROLINE I'm sorry.

SALLY Thanks to you we might not get planning permission. If you knew what this means to us –

CAROLINE But what about the village? What it means to the village?

SALLY The village is people too, you know. It's not just Cotswold stone and wooden beams and moss-covered walls. Keith's family has farmed here for five generations. You think we want to sell the spinney? You think we want that?

CAROLINE Then why do it?

SALLY You just don't get it, do you? Up there in the Rectory with your swimming pool and your ideas on everything that doesn't concern you. This isn't a matter of choice. I'm having another baby and we're desperate.

CAROLINE Well, having a baby is a choice.

SALLY *(beat)* How bloody typical.

CAROLINE I didn't mean –

SALLY Running around, shouting about wild flowers but when it comes to a human life –

CAROLINE That's not what I meant.

SALLY Isn't it?

CAROLINE I only meant –

SALLY What? What did you mean? You meant why don't you get rid of it, if it's inconvenient. Why don't you just get rid of it? I wish I could think like you. I really do. But I can't. I've got a family to look after. And that's exactly what I'm going to do.

Pause.

CAROLINE If it's a question of money...

SALLY *(beat)* You don't even know you're doing it, do you?

CAROLINE What?

Sally works on.

CAROLINE Is that for the sheep?

SALLY That's right.

CAROLINE Do you think you should be handling that stuff? I mean, when you're pregnant.

SALLY Why? You volunteering?

CAROLINE I just... It's potentially hazardous, that's all. For things like foetal development.

SALLY *(beat)* Everything's potentially hazardous if you use it wrong. We don't not use petrol cos it can be dangerous. We use it properly.

CAROLINE But have you read the warnings?

SALLY I know this'll come as a big surprise to you, Caroline, but us simple country folk do know what we're doing, you know.

Pause.

CAROLINE I hope this won't affect... I mean, the children are still welcome to use the pool.

SALLY They've a lot of homework this term.

CAROLINE Still...

SALLY You should get some kids of your own if you're so keen. You've too much time on your hands to poke your nose into other people's business.

CAROLINE *(beat)* I'm sorry you feel like that. But it's my business, too. It's everybody's business and if I don't take a stand, where will it end?

SALLY And if you do – where will it end then? *(Beat)* Why do you always think you know better than us?

CAROLINE Us?

SALLY Yes. Country people; people from the country;

who work in the country. This is our world.

Pause.

CAROLINE Sally –

SALLY I've got work to do.

Caroline goes. Sally spills some of chemicals on her hand and wipes her hand on her overalls.

SALLY Damn. *(The baby kicks, she realises her hand is on her belly, picks up the can and reads the warning.)* Oh, my God...

Before the hunt. We see John on the run.

David addresses the meet.

DAVID Ladies and gentlemen, if I could have your attention... First off, a big thanks to Sally and Keith for allowing us to meet here today and hunt over their land. As you know, this is the last hunt of the season and, I have decided, my last as Master. Events of recent months... personal... *(Beat)* Additionally, the changes forced upon us by certain sections of the 'community' – who frankly do not understand the ways of country people or the traditions they hold dear – have rather... Even now I expect we're being filmed and, if we do flush out a fox, Kenny will be forced to use the firearm. It's not how we'd have it but it's the law as it stands and it is for this reason also that I have decided to retire. *(Pause)* Thank you for your loyalty and support over the years and do please join me for a drink later at *The Star* where, I'm told, the Shepton Morris Men will be doing their stuff. Anyway, enough from me and here's to a change of government and a good day's hunting.

The hunt moves off. John runs...

Sally in her farmhouse.

SALLY I couldn't sleep. Kept thinking about what Caroline said about the chemicals. *(Beat)* You don't think to read all the warnings, do you? *(Beat)* And I was feeling a bit sick in any event so I got up to make a cup of tea and I was just sorting through some bills – it's amazing the stuff I get done in the night – and that's when I heard it. A single shot. Then another. And I thought about waking Keith, but he didn't get to bed while midnight, or calling the police but by the time they got here whoever it was would be long gone. So I put my coat on over my nightie – God knows what I thought I was going to do – and pulled on a pair of Keith's boots and went out. Be about two. And I was just turning by the old barn when I ran into him. Still carrying the gun. It was Bernard. And he looked at me and he said, 'You won't tell Keith, will you?' And I said, 'No.' And he said, 'I miss her so much.' And I took the gun off him – he just gave it to me – and I said, 'No more, eh?' And I put my arms round him... and that's not something I'd do normally cos he's not very touchy-feely, Bernard, and, to be honest, neither am I ... I put my arms round him and I held him. And he cried. Just like a little boy, really, and for the longest time. And then we came back to the house and I put the gun away and we both went back to bed. Mystery over.

The hunt gathers pace. John runs...

Patience at the station...

PATIENCE   If the train's on time I should be all right. I thought the eleventh hour of the eleventh day. *(Beat)* Not the eleventh month, obviously, you'd never get near the place and they might think I was going to assassinate someone. And I thought the Cenotaph because it's a memorial, isn't it, to all those who gave their lives so freely? Perhaps too freely. *(Beat)* 'Lest we forget.' But we have forgotten, haven't we? Or we pretend we don't know because we don't want to know because if we knew we'd have to do something about it. Like in Germany with the Jews. Or that prison camp in Cuba or wherever it is. Well, I know. *(Beat)* Right, have I got my Tupperware? *(checks)* Yes. Let's just hope it doesn't rain. I've no umbrella.

The hunt scents its prey. John hides.

Caroline in the spinney.

CAROLINE Apparently she isn't younger than me. He told me that as if it was supposed to make me feel better. It didn't. Apparently it just happened... working together, you know how it is. No, I said I didn't know. Apparently it's been going on for some time and I mustn't think it's a temporary infatuation or anything to do with our moving here, so bang goes that theory. And I can keep the house but he's going to sell the flat and move in with her. And her two kids. And I'll always be very special to him. Apparently. *(Beat)* Here they come.

Caroline videos the proceedings. The fox goes to ground.

David on horseback...

DAVID Well, if it isn't Madame Defarge.

CAROLINE David.

DAVID What, no knitting?

CAROLINE Difficult to manage when I'm holding the camcorder.

DAVID Of course, you wouldn't want to miss anything.

Pause.

DAVID There he goes, Kenny!

A gunshot, off...

DAVID Satisfied?

CAROLINE I just want to ensure no one is breaking the law.

DAVID Well, as you can see...

KENNY *(off)* Mr Haworth...

DAVID Did you get him?

KENNY You'd better come here, Mr Haworth.

DAVID *(going)* What is it?

The distant music of the Morris dance.

Sally enters.

SALLY   Caroline...

CAROLINE I'm a bit busy now.

SALLY   About those chemicals...

CAROLINE What?

SALLY   What else do you know?

David enters. Pause.

CAROLINE Has something happened?

DAVID   It's John. *(Beat)* He must have been hiding in the thicket and when Kenny used the shotgun...

SALLY   Oh, my God.

CAROLINE Is he –?

DAVID   Yes. I'm afraid so. *(Beat)* I'd better call the police.

SALLY   Thank God Patience isn't here.

DAVID   Yes. *(into phone)* Police please. *(To Caroline)* You'll have it all on film, I suppose. They'll want to see it.

Patience at the Cenotaph...

PATIENCE   I know some people might think it wrong but you could say Jesus committed suicide – well, he could've got out of it and he didn't – and what he did wasn't wrong, was it? He just wanted people to sit up and take notice and that's all I'm after doing. *(Beat)* Not that I'm comparing myself to Jesus – not with all the toffees I eat. Now how we doing? *(She checks her watch.)* Not bad. *(She holds her Tupperware box.)* I'll wait while the clock strikes.

DAVID *(into phone)* Oh yes. Yes, I'd like to report an accident.

Morris dancing music, off…

JOHN   For since by man came death, by man
came also the resurrection of the dead.
(*John emerges from the earth.*) And I saw a new
heaven and a new earth. And I, John, saw the holy
city. And he that sat upon the throne said: 'Behold
I make all things new.' And he said to me: 'It is
done. I am Alpha and Omega, the beginning and
the end.' And there came to me one of the Seven
Angels. And he showed me a pure river of the water
of life, clear as crystal. And on either side of the
river was the tree of life and the leaves of the tree
were for the healing of the nations. And I, John,
saw these things and heard them.'

During the above Patience takes the gun from the Tupperware box. Then, his speech finished, John begins to dance. But before the music ends he stops as a bell begins to strike eleven, far away. He looks up at the sky.

David, Caroline and Sally do likewise. Patience puts the gun in her mouth. David, Caroline and Sally look at one another. Sally feels the baby kick.

John looks at the audience.

The light goes but the music plays on…

The End.

MISSING IN ACTION

MISSING IN ACTION

Commissioned by Proteus Theatre Company and first performed at Central Studio, Queen Mary's College, Basingstoke on 5th October 2012, with the following cast:

CHARACTERS

Linda Yates	Ashley Christmas
Christopher Yates	Zoot Lynam
Darren (Spider) Webb	Paul Valentine
Vicky Adams	Louisa Quinn
Spider	Paul Huntley-Thomas
Ensemble (optional)	James Laurence Hunter
	Stuart Diamond
Director	Mary Swan
Designer	Sam Pine

For Proteus Theatre Company:

Artistic Director	Mary Swan

Thanks: to all those who talked to me in the course of my research: Victoria Tyrrell, Arthur James Pugh, Des & Jude Schweppe, Tony Gauvain, Bob Paxman, Richard Sharpe, Alan Rowe, Phil McAllister, Simon Chadderton, Gina Ralph, Gordon Hoggan, Elaine Laga, Michael Westhead, Graham Fearnall, Epeli Uluilakeba, Matthew Wadsworth and Nicole Chadwick. I was also greatly helped by a serving army officer who wishes to be nameless. Finally, big thanks to all at Proteus Theatre, and above all Mary, without whom...

Everyone Sang © Copyright Siegfried Sassoon by kind permission of the Estate of George Sassoon.

ACT ONE

Prelude

A clock strikes eleven. Linda and Vicky (a child in her arms) stand for the two minutes' silence.

From the back of the auditorium comes Spider, previously seen outside the venue, sleeping rough and drinking.

SPIDER   They went with songs to the battle, they
were young.
Straight of limb, true of eyes, steady and a-glow.
They were staunch to the end against odds uncounted,
They fell with their faces to the foe.
They shall grow not old, as we that are left
grow old:
Age shall not weary them, nor the years condemn.
At the going down of the sun and in the morning,
We will remember them.

A single cannon blast breaks the silence and the Last Post sounds.

LINDA   Every day's Remembrance Day for me. For Darren too I should think. Life's remembering now. It's like fog... You can walk through fog, can't you? Walk about and get things done, talk to people, laugh even – but you're always in the fog. It's the air you breathe. And it gets into your bones. You ache with it.

SPIDER   Lest we forget...

LINDA   The poppy wreathes, the band playing... 'Abide With Me'... We had that at his father's funeral. I'm glad John died before we lost him. I'm not sure he'd've coped.

SPIDER   The Glorious Dead...

LINDA   The memorial's beautiful, beautifully done... His name, carved with pride: Sapper Christopher Yates.

But where's the memorial to them as didn't die – or died later – hanged or overdosed or sat in car with a tube from the exhaust – and to them as are still fighting a war in their heads? To them that are missing?

SPIDER   Who remembers them, eh?

LINDA   Who remembers them?

Scene One

The boys at play.

CHRIS   And what have we got to lose?

DARREN   Er... Legs, arms, bollocks...

CHRIS   This was your idea.

DARREN   No it bloody wasn't!

CHRIS   All right, but like you say, what else is there?

DARREN   No bloody jobs round here.

CHRIS   Exactly. Whereas this way... get away from home... wages...

DARREN   Uniform!

CHRIS   The ladies love a uniform.

DARREN   Already got a lady, thank you.

CHRIS   Yeah, well, she'll love it.

DARREN   You reckon?

CHRIS   Learn to drive. Be a laugh.

DARREN   Something to do, I suppose.

CHRIS   That's what I'm saying!

DARREN   Together like?

CHRIS   Obviously.

DARREN	What'll your mum say?
CHRIS	She'll come round to it.
DARREN	What if she doesn't?
CHRIS	She will.

Interlude

The boys poring over army brochures.

SPIDER Think no more, lad; laugh, be jolly:
Why should men make haste to die?
Empty heads and tongues a-talking
Make the rough road easy walking,
And the feather pate of folly
Bears the falling sky.

Oh, 'tis jesting, dancing, drinking
Spins the heavy world around.
If young hearts were not so clever
Oh, they would be young for ever:
Think no more; 'tis only tinking
Lays lads underground.

CHRIS	So? What do you reckon?
DARREN	Yeah.
CHRIS	Yeah?
DARREN	Yeah!
CHRIS	Yeah!!
DARREN	Like you say. What have we got to lose?

Scene Two

Linda pegging out / folding washing. The boys still tearing about.

LINDA   Tweedle-dum and Tweedle-dee. Double trouble. First day of school they met. Reception class, St George's. And after that... Well, he was a bit of a fixture, Darren. Playing over, staying over. Spider, Chris calls him – with his name being Webb. Came on holiday with us more than once. John'd take 'em both to football, swimming... although we'd to buy Darren trunks cos she'd sent him round with just his underpants. I'm not criticising. She wasn't well a lot of the time and his dad... I don't think he knew what to do – liked a drink. Or maybe he didn't like it but anyway, he drank. I'm not saying they didn't love him... and he could be a little bugger, Darren. Mind, our Christopher was no angel. Expect that's why they got on.

They did fall out one time – came to blows I think – but it was soon mended. Best mates again and off on one of their trips. Wales, I think it was. Cockle picking. Something ... They had all the gear. Even when they were little, John'd rig up a tent in the garden, back garden, and they'd play in there all day, sleep there in the summer. Always doing... always up to something.

And when John died... Chris was only fourteen... went off the rails a bit. Trouble with the police, drinking, smoking stuff. I could've done with some of it myself. Anyway, it was Darren brought him round, really. I think with him having lost his mum, you know, he knew what Chris was going through... Good lads, the pair of them... Not that they did much at school. Apart from sport. So what they're going to do now they've left, God alone knows.

CHRIS *(entering)* We've joined up!

LINDA   What?

CHRIS   The Army –

DARREN   Royal Engineers!

CHRIS   Yeah!

LINDA   Joined up?

CHRIS   Yeah, you know – joined up!

LINDA *(beat)* You're not old enough.

CHRIS   We are.

DARREN   Well…

CHRIS   We need you to say. I do.

LINDA   And is this you, an' all, Darren?

DARREN   Yeah!

LINDA   Does your dad know?

DARREN   Er…

LINDA   And Vicky, have you told her?

DARREN   Er…

LINDA   So how long have you been planning this?

DARREN   Ages.

CHRIS   No. A bit. And we've not been 'planning' it.

DARREN   We have.

CHRIS   No, not like… Makes it sounds like we went behind your back.

LINDA   And didn't you?

CHRIS   I thought you'd be pleased.

DARREN   No, you said –

CHRIS   Spider!

LINDA   Thank you, Darren.

CHRIS   Yeah, thanks a bunch!

LINDA   Leave him alone! *(Beat)* So what's brought this on?

CHRIS   How d'you −?

LINDA   Putting your name down for the army?

DARREN   Royal Engineers.

LINDA   I heard you the first time, thank you, Darren.

CHRIS   It's a good job.

LINDA   It's a bit more than that!

CHRIS   Well, there aren't any others, are there?

DARREN   He's right, Mrs Yates. And you get to learn to drive.

CHRIS   Yeah, they teach you to drive.

LINDA   You can learn to drive... Don't have to join the bloody army to do that.

DARREN   But tanks and that!

LINDA   Tanks?

CHRIS   So you going to pay for lessons?

LINDA   How can I afford driving lessons? Can hardly pay the mortgage.

CHRIS   Exactly! This is win-win... don't you see? You won't have to keep me, feed me − can get a lodger, rent my room out. Might even be able to send you something.

DARREN   And me!

LINDA   Oh, Darren, don't be −

CHRIS   So?

LINDA *(beat)* You won't last five minutes.

CHRIS   We will.

DARREN   We will.

LINDA *(beat)* You can't lie in bed half the morning. It's all discipline in the army, you know, and keep fit.

DARREN   Phys.

LINDA   What?

DARREN   They call it phys.

LINDA   Do they?

DARREN   ...Yeah.

LINDA *(beat)* And you think you could hack it, do you?

CHRIS   Yeah.

DARREN   Yeah.

LINDA *(beat)* And it's what you want?

CHRIS   Yeah.

DARREN   Yeah.

LINDA *(beat)* I don't know... There's lads getting killed every day, injured –

CHRIS   Not –

LINDA   Don't tell me, it's on the news! You think I want to wave you off to get you back in a box?

CHRIS   I knew you'd be like this!

LINDA   And what's that?

CHRIS   This. All negative.

LINDA   Oh, is that what I'm being? I bet the bloke at the recruitment place –

DARREN   Sergeant.

LINDA   I bet he didn't read you the casualty figures, did he?

CHRIS   He did actually.

DARREN   Did he?

LINDA   Course he didn't. Not going to read you the names of the glorious dead, is he?

CHRIS   It's part of being a soldier.

DARREN   Serving your country.

CHRIS   Laying down your life if necessary.

LINDA   And you're prepared to do that, are you?

CHRIS   Yeah.

DARREN   Yeah.

LINDA *(beat)* God help us: they must've seen you coming.

CHRIS *(beat)* Dad'd've let me.

LINDA   He bloody wouldn't – not if he'd wanted to find me here when he got home.

DARREN   My dad won't give a bugger. Glad to get rid of me.

LINDA   And that's another thing. You're going to leave me, are you? It's not enough losing your father but I have to lose you now!

CHRIS   No-one's losing anyone. You get loads of leave and that.

DARREN   Well...

CHRIS   I'll be back before you know it.

LINDA   I've not said yes yet.

DARREN   I'll look after him, Mrs Yates.

LINDA   Is that right?

DARREN   Always. Promise.

LINDA *(beat)* And that'll be enough, will it?

CHRIS   We'll look out for each other.

DARREN   Yeah.

LINDA *(beat)* I don't know... I'll have to think about it...

CHRIS   But you'll say yes?

LINDA   Think about it, I said!

Interlude

Chris is following Linda about.

SPIDER   Oh stay at home, my lad, and plough
The Land and not the sea,
And leave the soldiers at their drill,
And all about the idle hill
Shepherd your sheep with me.

Oh stay with company and mirth
And daylight and the air;
Too full already is the grave
Of fellows that were good and brave
And died because they were.

CHRIS   Well?

LINDA   You're sure this is what you want?

CHRIS   Yes!

LINDA   All right then.

CHRIS   Yes!

Chris and Darren celebrate.
Spider drinks.

Scene Three

Darren and Vicky...

VICKY   And what about us?

DARREN   What about us?

VICKY   Where does this leave us?

DARREN   Doesn't leave us anywhere.

VICKY   Thanks very much!

DARREN   No, I mean – I don't mean – I mean – it doesn't change anything.

VICKY   You don't think so?

DARREN   Why should it change anything?

VICKY   Darren!

DARREN   What?

VICKY   Only that you'll be one end of the country and I'll be here.

DARREN   Yeah... But not forever. Just a few months.

VICKY   Oh, and then what?

DARREN   That depends.

VICKY   On what?

DARREN   Where they send you.

VICKY   Exactly.

DARREN   Could be Germany.

VICKY   Germany?

DARREN   Different places.

VICKY   Like Afghanistan.

DARREN   That's not a posting. That's a tour of duty.

VICKY   And the difference is?

DARREN   The difference is that on a tour of duty – say Afghanistan – I'm there for a few months –

VICKY   Getting killed.

DARREN   No!

VICKY   Pah!

DARREN   Do you know the statistics for how many people get killed and that?

VICKY   No, do you?

DARREN *(beat)* No, but it's not that many – not when you think of how many troops we've got out there.

VICKY   Is this what they told you?

DARREN   No.

VICKY   It is, isn't it?

DARREN   So what if it is? My point is – the odds are, nothing's going to happen. And anyway, that's a tour of duty but on a posting –

VICKY   To Germany!

DARREN   Well, it might be Germany or it might be somewhere else.

VICKY   Like where?

DARREN   I don't know, like Devon or somewhere.

VICKY   Devon?

DARREN   I don't know! But the point is, wherever it is, wherever I am, wherever they send me, you'll be there too.

VICKY   And how do you figure that?

DARREN   That's what I'm saying. That's the whole point – well, not the whole point but anyway, what I'm saying is – it's a job isn't it? A secure job and this way we can be together.

VICKY *(beat)* Is that a proposal?

DARREN   No. I'm just saying.

VICKY   Are you proposing?

DARREN   No. I just mean, say, some time in the future, if that's what we want, if that's what we both want then... Yeah, alright then, yeah, if you like, yeah, it's a proposal.

VICKY   Aren't you supposed to get down on one knee?

DARREN   Aren't you supposed to be not so bloody awkward?

VICKY   Thanks a lot!

DARREN   Just saying.

Pause.

VICKY   What if you get shot or something?

DARREN   I won't.

VICKY   Or blown up?

DARREN   I won't!

VICKY   But what if you do?

DARREN   Bloody hell, I've not even joined up yet!

VICKY *(beat)* And this is both of you, is it?

DARREN   Yeah.

VICKY   And what does your Dad say?

DARREN   Who cares?

VICKY   And Chris's mum? What did she say?

DARREN   She's all in favour. Thinks it's great.

VICKY   You're such a liar.

DARREN   No!

VICKY *(beat)* Anyhow, you won't stick it.

DARREN   I bloody will.

VICKY   You bloody won't.

DARREN   How much d'you bet?

VICKY   A fiver.

DARREN   Right. You're on.

VICKY   That's a fiver you owe me.

DARREN   In your dreams!

They embrace.

CHRIS *(to Darren)* Come on!

LINDA *(to Vicky)* You too!

Interlude

The sound of recruits training. The boys change into combat gear and the girls into their glad rags.

DARREN   I loved it, me. Bloody loved it.

CHRIS   But Corporal Maxwell –

DARREN   Mad Max! -

CHRIS   Never heard anyone shout –

DARREN   Or swear –

CHRIS   So much.

SPIDER   Right then! Move it!

The boys run on the spot.

CHRIS   They taught you how to iron.

DARREN   How to shave.

CHRIS   I didn't need to shave – didn't have anything to shave – but they still taught you.

DARREN   How to make your beds.

CHRIS   How to shower proper!

DARREN   Even how to wash your –

VICKY   All right, Darren, we get the picture!

LINDA   Course we did have a few tears...

CHRIS   No we didn't!

DARREN   Come on, mate.

CHRIS   No.

DARREN   Mate, we all did. I did. Cried my eyes out one time.

CHRIS   Did you?

DARREN   Missing Vicky.

VICKY *(throwing him a present)* Happy birthday!

CHRIS   You never said.

DARREN   Well, I wasn't cracking on, was I? Not after the stick you got.

CHRIS   Oh, thank you!

SPIDER   On your belt buckle!

BOYS   Yes, Corporal!

The boys hit the deck.

LINDA   Bit of a cliché, I know, but it really did make a man of him.

VICKY   And Darren.

LINDA   Although why they have to cut their hair so short, I don't know. And he's got lovely hair, our Christopher.

DARREN   Aw!

CHRIS   Mum!

LINDA   Well, you have!

SPIDER   Right! On your feet!

BOYS   Yes, Corporal!

The boys stand.

LINDA   And why they have to shout so much!

VICKY   I know!

DARREN   You should hear the bloody Sergeant!

LINDA	You'd wonder they don't loose their voices!
CHRIS	Believe me, they don't!
SPIDER	Fix bayonets! *(The boys do so.)*
LINDA	There's bits they don't tell you.
VICKY	Didn't want to know, me.
SPIDER	Spirit of the bayonet?
BOYS	Kill, kill, kill!
SPIDER	What makes the grass grow?
BOYS	Blood, blood, blood!
LINDA	But I suppose they have to do it.
VICKY	Suppose.

SPIDER On guard! *(The boys assume the position.)* I want to see it in your eyes. Want to see you want to kill these fuckers! See those dummies? That's the fucking Taliban. Just killed some of your mates. You want to fucking kill 'em, right?

BOYS	Yes, Corporal.
SPIDER	You want to fucking kill 'em.
BOYS	Yes, Corporal.
SPIDER	Can't hear you!
BOYS	Yes, Corporal!
SPIDER	Show me your war face!

The boys roar and charge off.

LINDA	I never thought they'd stick it.
VICKY	Me neither.
LINDA	I mean Chris likes his sport and that.
VICKY	Cost me a fiver!
LINDA	But he also likes his bed!
VICKY	Still, some bets you don't mind losing!

The girls fix their make-up and the boys change into dress uniform.

SPIDER   If you can keep your head when all about you
Are losing theirs and blaming it on you;
If you can trust yourself when all men doubt you,
But make allowance for their doubting too:
If you can wait and not be tired by waiting,
Or being lied about, don't deal in lies,
Or being hated don't give way to hating,
And yet don't look too good, nor talk too wise;

If you can dream — and not make dreams your master;
If you can think — and not make thoughts your aim,
If you can meet with Triumph and Disaster
And treat those two impostors just the same:
If you can bear to hear the truth you've spoken
Twisted by knaves to make a trap for fools,
Or watch the things you gave your life to, broken,
And stoop and build 'em up with worn-out tools;

If you can make one heap of all your winnings
And risk it on one turn of pitch-and-toss,
And lose, and start again at your beginnings
And never breathe a word about your loss:
If you can force your heart and nerve and sinew
To serve your turn long after they are gone,
And so hold on when there is nothing in you
Except the Will which says to them: 'Hold on!'

If you can talk with crowds and keep your virtue,
Or walk with Kings — nor lose the common touch,
If neither foes nor loving friends can hurt you,
If all men count with you, but none too much:
If you can fill the unforgiving minute
With sixty seconds' worth of distance run,
Yours is the Earth and everything that's in it,
And — which is more — you'll be a Man, my son!

LINDA   It was a wonderful day.

VICKY   Fantastic!

LINDA   You get there and they treat you like royalty.

VICKY   All the officers and that, all in uniform!

LINDA   Everyone dressed to the nines.

VICKY   Like a wedding.

LINDA   But not so competitive.

VICKY   These shoes are killing me.

LINDA   Mine too.

VICKY   And you're all in a stand, like, waiting.

LINDA   And there's flags and great big guns all over the place.

VICKY   And then you hear it.

And we hear the band: Dur - dur - dum! Dur - dur - dum!

VICKY   And the band comes marching round the corner!

LINDA   And there they are!

VICKY   Marching.

LINDA   And you're looking to spot your boy. Which one?

VICKY   They all look amazing.

LINDA   So smart!

VICKY   All in lines like, eyes front.

LINDA   And then!

SPIDER   By the right... Eyes right!

The boys turn to face their audience.

VICKY   There they are!

LINDA   Your baby... A soldier!

Cheering and kissing and photographs being taken and Spider watching as the boys wrap themselves in the Union Jack.

Scene Four

SPIDER   Yours is the Earth and everything that's in it,
And – which is more – you'll be a Man, my son!

The cheers fade away.

LINDA   Look at you! *(Chris grins)* I wish your dad could see you. He'd be so proud.

CHRIS   You think?

LINDA   I know. *(Beat)* Your dad couldn't make it then, Darren?

DARREN   No.

LINDA   No, well... Never mind. You can show him the pictures.

DARREN   Yeah...

Linda takes a photo.

VICKY *(to Darren)* Did you get them?

DARREN   Wearing them, aren't I?

LINDA   What's that?

DARREN   Er...

CHRIS   Nothing. Anyhow, we did it, eh?

LINDA   Yes, you did. I'm so proud of you. The pair of you.

CHRIS   Thanks, mum.

VICKY   Yeah.

DARREN   Proudest day of my life!

Interlude

VOICEOVER   Families and friends of Thirty-four Engineer Regiment deploying to Afghanistan have been briefed on what to expect when they are separated for the duration of a six-month tour in the next few weeks.

Lt Col Philpot said the Family Day briefing satisfied a thirst for knowledge, unequalled in past years, about the details of the imminent tour and helped ensure as many people as possible were given details of welfare and support...

They look at one another and get out of their glad rags as Spider sings.

SPIDER   Brother Bertie went away
To do his bit the other day
With a smile on his lips and his Lieutenant's pips
Upon his shoulder bright and gay

As the train moved out he said,
'Remember me to all the birds.'
Then he wagged his paw and went away to war
Shouting out these pathetic words:

Goodbye-ee, goodbye-ee,
Wipe the tear, baby dear, from your eye-ee,
Tho' it's hard to part I know,
I'll be tickled to death to go.

Don't cry-ee, dont sigh-ee,
there's a silver lining in the sky-ee,
Bonsoir, old thing, cheer-i-o, chin, chin,
Nah-poo, toodle-oo, Goodbye-ee.

Spider picks up the abandoned flag.

Scene Five

Linda and Chris / Vicky and Darren

LINDA	Have you got everything?
CHRIS	Yeah.
LINDA	Sure?
CHRIS	Yeah.
LINDA	All your extra stuff, the stuff you bought.
CHRIS	I've got it, yeah.
VICKY	Going to miss you.
DARREN	Going to miss you too.
VICKY	Phone, yeah?
DARREN	When they let us.
VICKY	Don't matter what time.
DARREN	Won't have to.
LINDA	What about pants?
CHRIS	Pants?
LINDA	Have you got enough pants?
CHRIS	Yeah.
LINDA	I bought you these just in case.
CHRIS	Oh.
LINDA	Don't you like them?
CHRIS	No, it's...
LINDA	What?
CHRIS	I think I've got enough pants, mum.
LINDA	You sure?
CHRIS	Yeah, honest.

DARREN   You know what I'd really like?

VICKY   What? *(He whispers in her ear.)* No!

DARREN   Go on!

VICKY   No way!

DARREN   You did it for Passing Out.

VICKY   Not the ones I was wearing!

LINDA   Well, do you want to take them for Darren?

CHRIS   I don't think Darren wants you buying him pants.

LINDA   Why not?

CHRIS   Look, I think we're both fine on the pants front.

LINDA   Well there's some Nutella, Twiglets – them's for Darren, don't you go eating them – and Mini Eggs for you.

CHRIS   Mini Eggs?

LINDA   I thought they wouldn't melt you know, with it being so hot.

CHRIS   Oh. Right.

LINDA   Give us a kiss then.

CHRIS   I'll be back in a few months.

LINDA   I know! Just giving my son a kiss. If you don't mind!

CHRIS   I do actually.

DARREN   Give us a kiss.

Kisses all round.

LINDA   And make sure you let me know how you are. Both of you. And tell me the truth. I'll know if you're lying. And take care, won't you?

CHRIS   Course.

LINDA	Right then.
CHRIS	And will you be all right?
LINDA	Me? Yeah. Course I will.
CHRIS	Right then.
LINDA	Right.
DARREN	Better be off.
VICKY	Yeah.
DARREN	Yeah.
LINDA	Go on, then.
CHRIS	Right.
LINDA	Yeah.
VICKY	Wish you weren't going.
DARREN	No choice.
CHRIS	You will be all right?
LINDA	Just go, will you!
CHRIS	All right! I'm going.
LINDA	Be careful, yeah?
DARREN	Don't worry, Mrs Yates, I'll look after him!
LINDA	See you do! And yourself...
VICKY	Love you.
DARREN	Love you.
CHRIS	Love you.
LINDA	Oh, go on!

Lights down.

ACT TWO

Prelude

The women packing shoe boxes with gifts for the boys.

SPIDER Don't cry-ee, dont sigh-ee,
there's a silver lining in the sky-ee,
Bonsoir, old thing, cheer-i-o, chin, chin,
Nah-poo, toodle-oo, Goodbye-ee...

LINDA It's like when they first go to school or you watch them cross the road on their own... You don't breathe. From the minute they go to the day they come home on leave, and you can see them – see they're in one piece and give them a cuddle, cos they never stop being your baby, do they? You don't really ever breathe. I didn't. Not properly.

VICKY Course you get on with things... the world doesn't stop, does it? But there's always a bit of you... I don't know how to describe it... outside looking in... something. And you try not to go anywhere you don't have a signal in case he phones and you've got the MOD website as your home page and last thing at night, first thing in the morning you're on there checking for news, hoping there isn't any.

LINDA And if you hear on the radio there's been another fatality you wait for the words: 'the family has been told' – because then you know it's not your lad. And you're relieved and guilty at the same time, cos if it's not your son, it's someone else's isn't it?

VICKY Or boyfriend. Or brother. Or father. That must be terrible. How do you tell kiddies their dad's not coming back?

LINDA So you keep yourself busy. And you send them bits and bobs, daft stuff, stuff they can't get over there. Things they like, little luxuries – anything to make life a bit more, you know...

Scene Six

The boys in Afghanistan.

DARREN   Twiglets! Brilliant!

CHRIS   Nutella.... Mini Eggs

DARREN   She's a bloody genius your mum.

CHRIS   Oh, no!

DARREN   What?

CHRIS   She's only gone and sent me...

DARREN   What?

CHRIS   She's obsessed!

DARREN   What with?

CHRIS   Bloody underpants.

DARREN   Well, you can never have too many.

CHRIS   Don't you start!

DARREN   What?

CHRIS   Oh, and you'd wear them, would you?

DARREN   Don't need to. Got my own!

And he displays a pair of Vicky's pants.

CHRIS   I hope they're clean!

DARREN   I hope they're not!

CHRIS   You dirty bastard!

DARREN   I will be when I get five minutes!

The boys enjoy their treats.

DARREN   If you had to lose something, what would it be? Would you rather lose your arms or legs?

CHRIS   Dunno... Think I could take any injury, long as

I survived.

DARREN   Mm... I think legs are over-rated.

CHRIS   How do you work that out?

DARREN   Lose your legs, you can get new ones, can't you? Carbon fucking fibre – like that runner. South African. And all that compensation! You'd be loaded if you lost your legs. No more worries on the money front!

CHRIS   Bloody hell!

DARREN   But your arms... No... Or being paralysed from the neck down... Don't think I could handle that. I mean what would you do about..?

CHRIS   You've given this some serious thought, then?

DARREN   Or your bollocks. Imagine losing your bollocks!

CHRIS (*about to eat a Mini Egg but thinking better of it*) Do you think we could talk about something else?

DARREN   Just saying.

CHRIS   Well, don't.

Pause.

DARREN   I could tell you about my dream.

CHRIS   Oh yeah?

DARREN   I had this dream.

CHRIS   Do I want to hear this?

DARREN   Not like that!

CHRIS   Like what then?

DARREN   There's Vicky right –

CHRIS   I thought you said –

DARREN   No, listen... She's only got a baby!

CHRIS   And whose is that?

DARREN   Mine, you cheeky bastard!

CHRIS   All right, just asking! *(Beat)* Is that it?

DARREN   No. You're there an' all.

CHRIS   And what am I doing?

DARREN   Wait. And your mum. Except she's my mum in the dream.

CHRIS   Right...

DARREN   And some bloke.

CHRIS   Who?

DARREN   God knows, some down and out. And the weird thing is –

CHRIS   You mean it's not weird so far?

DARREN   Just listen, dick head.

CHRIS   I'm all ears.

DARREN   We're like... birds.

CHRIS   Birds?

DARREN   Yeah. And what's even weirder –

CHRIS   It gets weirder?

DARREN   We're all... singing.

CHRIS   Right.

DARREN   But not like birds. You know, like people.

CHRIS   Right.

DARREN   Cos there's music.

CHRIS   Course there is. Anything else?

DARREN   Well, we're flying, obviously –

CHRIS   Obviously.

DARREN   More like gliding, really – soaring.

CHRIS   Right.

DARREN   But we're *really* asleep.

CHRIS   OK. So we're a flock of singing, flying –

DARREN   Soaring –

CHRIS   – birds who are really asleep.

DARREN   Yeah.

CHRIS   Right.

DARREN   Is that mad, do you think?

CHRIS   No mate. No, it's not – course it's bloody mad! What kind of a dream's that?

DARREN   I'm telling you the dream I had. I don't know what kind it is! Bloody hell, I won't bother next time.

CHRIS   You soft bastard.

DARREN   I'll tell you what though: it was bloody beautiful!

Darren grins. They both grin.

DARREN   Out on patrol tomorrow.

CHRIS   Yeah.

DARREN   Like the fucking A Team.

CHRIS   Fucking Terminator.

DARREN   Fucking Rambo!

CHRIS   Yeah...

DARREN *(beat)* I'm cacking myself.

CHRIS   Me too.

DARREN *(beat)* Just as well your mum sent them pants then.

The boys laugh.

Interlude

The sound of an explosion.

SPIDER   I need a medic!

VO   There are reports from Afghanistan of an incident involving ISAF troops and Taliban Insurgents in Helmand province that has resulted in the loss of civilian lives. Several members of one family, including children, are believed to be amongst the casualties.

We see Darren carrying the dead child, an image that will recur at other points in the play, although sometimes Darren will be carrying his own child or Chris.

Scene Seven

Chris with Linda / Darren with Vicky.

LINDA   Oh come here! Let me give you a love! *(She does so.)* Have you lost weight? You've lost weight!

CHRIS   I've no idea.

LINDA   Are they feeding you properly? Are you getting enough to eat?

CHRIS   Yes! It's forty in the shade over there, remember.

LINDA   Well, I hope you're drinking plenty of water.

CHRIS   Course I am or I wouldn't be here, would I?

LINDA   Oh, let me have a look at you! *(She does so.)* You've definitely lost weight.

CHRIS   All right, so I've lost weight!

LINDA   And how's Darren? Is he all right?

CHRIS   Yeah... Yeah. You know Spider. Straight round to Vicky's.

LINDA   She's really missed him.

CHRIS   That makes two of them. Surprised we can't hear the bed springs from here.

LINDA   Christopher!

CHRIS   What?

LINDA   You're not in the barrack room now.

CHRIS   In the where?

LINDA   I don't know! Wherever it is you talk like that.

CHRIS   Bloody hell!

Pause.

LINDA *(looking at him)* Oh! *(Beat)* So?

CHRIS   So?

LINDA   Tell me!

CHRIS   What?

LINDA   Oh, you are annoying!

CHRIS   Told you on the phone.

LINDA   I bet!

CHRIS   What then?

LINDA   What happened when what's-his-name went over?

CHRIS   Oh, that was a joke. It's the same whenever one of them decides to roll up. Everything has to stop – all the work you're actually there to do – that all stops so you can cover their arses. If they really wanted to *show support for the lads* they wouldn't come in the first place. But they all want their photos took, poncing about in a flak jacket.

LINDA *(beat)* Is it scary?

CHRIS   No. *(Beat)* Sometimes. Some of it.

LINDA   It looks so desolate when you see it on the news.

CHRIS   No it's... When you're on early stag... the dawn like... the colours... Amazing. And the Afghans – not the Taliban, obviously, we hate them bastards – but the ordinary people, they're just, you know... And the kids... cheeky little sods!

LINDA   We heard about those kiddies being killed.

CHRIS   Yeah.

LINDA   Terrible that.

CHRIS   Yeah... Stuff happens sometimes.

LINDA   I know but – You weren't involved, were you?

CHRIS   No.

LINDA   You'd tell me, wouldn't you?

CHRIS   Yeah.

LINDA   So you weren't?

CHRIS   No!

LINDA   No. Sorry. It's just... I worry.

CHRIS   Well don't. I'm fine. We're both fine.

LINDA   I can't help it.

CHRIS   No point worrying. It's my job, what I do.

LINDA   And worrying's what I do. Oh, come here!

She embraces him.

CHRIS   Bloody hell!

Darren and Vicky after sex.

DARREN   Sorry.

VICKY   No, it's all right.

DARREN   It's not though, is it?

VICKY   It's just... You're not normally so...

DARREN   I didn't mean it, honest.

VICKY   No well next time... Just   take it a bit slower, yeah?

DARREN   Sorry.

VICKY   I'm not going anywhere.

DARREN   No. No. Sorry.

Pause.

VICKY   Missed you so much.

DARREN   Did you?

VICKY   Course I did! Didn't you miss me?

DARREN   Course.

VICKY   You didn't phone as much the last few weeks.

DARREN   I did, didn't I? Didn't I? Sorry. It gets a bit mad sometimes. Don't feel like talking. Just want to get some scran and get your head down.

VICKY   But you're all right?

DARREN   Course I am. Why wouldn't I be?

VICKY   Don't know. You just seem...

DARREN   What?

VICKY   A bit... Jumpy.

DARREN   Just a bit of a mind fuck coming back. I mean yesterday, we're out on patrol – you're like totally alert – totally, and today here I am. With you.

VICKY   Suppose that is a bit mad.

DARREN   Yeah.

VICKY   Probably just tired.

DARREN   Yeah. *(Beat)* Might go for a run.

VICKY   Run?

DARREN   Yeah.

VICKY   Thought you were –

DARREN   What?

VICKY   No. Nothing.

DARREN *(beat)* Sorry about before...

VICKY   Go on, then...

DARREN   Get my stuff...

VICKY   Yeah.

They kiss. He goes. Vicky wonders...

LINDA   Did you get them pants I sent?

CHRIS   I did. Yeah.

LINDA   Were they all right?

CHRIS   I haven't really worn 'em yet.

LINDA   Why not?

CHRIS   I've been... saving them... for best. *(Beat)* You were right about the Mini Eggs though.

LINDA   See! Mother knows best!

CHRIS   Will the water be hot, do you think?

LINDA   Should be by now. If it's not playing up again.

CHRIS   I'll go and have a shower then.

LINDA   I got you some of that gel you like.

CHRIS   Brilliant.

LINDA   And then I'll do you some tea and you can tell me all your news.

CHRIS   Oh... Said I'd meet Darren.

LINDA   You only saw him this morning!

CHRIS   I know but... Said we'd get some scoff, go for a drink. *(Beat)* We're home for a week.

LINDA *(beat)* Well, be careful.

CHRIS   We've just been in Afghan!

LINDA   That's what I mean. You know what people are like. Go looking for trouble, some of them.

CHRIS   I think we can handle ourselves!

He goes.

Interlude

The boys on the town.

SPIDER   I went into a public-'ouse to get a pint o' beer,
The publican 'e up an' sez, *We serve no red-coats here.*
The girls be'ind the bar they laughed an' giggled fit to die,
I outs into the street again an' to myself sez I:
O it's Tommy this, an' Tommy that, an' *Tommy, go away*;
But it's *Thank you, Mister Atkins*, when the band begins to play,
The band begins to play, my boys, the band begins to play,
O it's *Thank you, Mister Atkins*, when the band begins to play.
(Darren is drunk, shouting and swearing at unseen provokers.)
Yes, makin' mock o' uniforms that guard you while you sleep
Is cheaper than them uniforms, an' they're starvation cheap;

An' hustlin' drunken soldiers when they're goin'
large a bit
Is five times better business than paradin' in full kit.
Then it's Tommy this, an' Tommy that, an' *Tommy,
'ow's yer soul?*
But it's *Thin red line of 'eroes* when the drums
begin to roll,
The drums begin to roll, my boys, the drums begin
to roll,
O it's *Thin red line of 'eroes* when the drums begin
to roll.
(*It's all Chris can do to get him away before they
get into a fight.*)
You talk o' better food for us, an' schools, an' fires,
an' all:
We'll wait for extra rations if you treat us rational.
Don't mess about the cook-room slops, but prove it
to our face
The Widow's Uniform is not the soldier-man's
disgrace.
For it's Tommy this, an' Tommy that, an' *Chuck
him out, the brute!*
But it's *Saviour of 'is country* when the guns begin
to shoot;
An' it's Tommy this, an' Tommy that, an' anything
you please;
An' Tommy ain't a bloomin' fool—you bet that
Tommy sees!

Scene Eight

In sick bay.

CHRIS   You still here, then?

DARREN   What's it look like?

CHRIS   How you feeling?

BIG THEATRE IN SMALL SPACES

DARREN	Shit.
CHRIS	What did the medics say?
DARREN	Stay in bed, take these tablets, lots of water bla, bla.
CHRIS	Jammy bastard.
DARREN	Wouldn't say that if you had it.

Pause.

CHRIS	Got something for you.
DARREN	What is it?
CHRIS	Present from my mum.
DARREN	What?

He produces a bag of Twiglets.

CHRIS	Da-dah!
DARREN	Oh. No, ta.
CHRIS	No to Twiglets? You must be bloody ill.
DARREN	I bloody am!
CHRIS	All right. Chill. *(Beat)* What is it? You've been like this for weeks.
DARREN	Like what?
CHRIS	This! All...
DARREN	Oh, and how the fuck would you know?
CHRIS	Me? Let me think... Oh, yeah: I know! Cos I'm your mate, that's why – your best mate – known you since you were a kid and I know what you're like and it's not like this. What is it? Eh? *(Beat)* Before we went home you couldn't wait to get there and the minute we're there, you couldn't wait to get back.
DARREN	So...
CHRIS	What's that mean?

DARREN   Bunch of twats... Stupid bloody questions: *Did you kill anyone?*

CHRIS   I know.

DARREN   What they expect you to say? *Oh, yeah mate, do it all the time, all in a day's work to me!* They've no idea. No idea of the shit we have to go through.

CHRIS   All right!

Pause.

DARREN   Keep thinking about that kid.

CHRIS   Yeah...

DARREN   And Vicky doesn't want to know. Try to tell her anything, she changes the subject.

CHRIS   Well, you can't have it both ways! My mum's the exact opposite, wants a blow by blow account. Like you would.

DARREN   No fucking idea.

CHRIS   Well, did we before we got here? Remember all the bollocks in the recruitment videos: travel the world! Be part of a team!

DARREN   Yeah!

CHRIS   Whereas the reality, as we now know is –

DARREN   Eat from a bag, sleep in a bag –

CHRIS   Shit in a bag! Exactly.

DARREN   Talking of which... You still got them pants your mum sent you?

CHRIS   Yeah, why?

DARREN   Might need 'em myself at this rate.

CHRIS   Well, wiping your arse is about all they're fit for.

DARREN   Ungrateful bastard.

CHRIS   I know.

SPIDER   Yatesy! Time for walkies!

CHRIS   This should be you, you lazy bastard.

DARREN   I hope you get it. Then you'll know!

CHRIS   No chance. Guts of steel, me.

DARREN   Yeah, yeah.

CHRIS   Want me to get you anything?

DARREN   No, I'm fine.

CHRIS   See you later then.

DARREN   Actually, there is something.

CHRIS   What?

DARREN   If you go in my bag.

CHRIS   I'm not touching those knickers!

DARREN   Fuck off!

SPIDER   Yatesy!

CHRIS   What then?

DARREN   At the bottom, there's a book.

CHRIS   Book, you?

DARREN   All right!

CHRIS (*producing the book*) *The Soldier's Song?*

DARREN   It was my mum's, all right?

CHRIS   What is it?

DARREN   Poetry and that.

CHRIS   You soft bastard!

DARREN   I haven't read it!

CHRIS   What you want it for, then?

DARREN   Just give it here, will you?

He does so.

CHRIS   Sure I can't tempt you?

DARREN   No.

He opens the Twiglets and eats.

CHRIS   Oh well, keep taking the tablets.

DARREN   Yeah, right. Fuck off.

CHRIS   Love you too!

SPIDER   We'll be going without you!

CHRIS   I wish! You get your head down. See you later.

DARREN   You better.

Chris goes. Darren holds his book and sleeps.

Interlude

SPIDER   When the 'arf-made recruity goes out to the East
'E acts like a babe an' 'e drinks like a beast,
An' 'e wonders because 'e is frequent deceased
Ere 'e's fit for to serve as a soldier, a soldier,
Ere 'e's fit for to serve as a soldier.

VICKY *(with a pregnancy test)* Replace cap... Windows facing up... Positive results may be observed in one minute or less depending on the level of hCG. *(Beat)* Right...

SPIDER   Now the worst o' your foes is the sun over'ead:
You must wear your 'elmet for all that is said:
If 'e finds you uncovered 'e'll knock you down dead,
An' you'll die like a fool of a soldier, a soldier,
An' you'll die like a fool of a soldier.

LINDA   I know he doesn't like me buying him clothes but I saw this in the catalogue and I thought you can't really go wrong with a track-suit, can you? Well, you probably can but

I got it anyway and I think I'll be alright cos it's the same make as the trainers he bought just before he went. Anyway, if he turns his nose up, I can send it back. One more week... And then I can breathe...

SPIDER When first under fire an' you're wishful to duck,
Don't look nor take 'eed at the man that is struck,
Be thankful you're livin', and trust to your luck
And march to your front like a soldier, a soldier,
And march to your front like a soldier.

VICKY It's almost worse as the tour gets towards the end. When he first went, it was horrible. Missed him – obviously – and kept thinking about things he must be seeing. But then when he came home on leave I wanted to ask him and at the same time I didn't because I wasn't sure if it was better to know or not know, you know. And now, these last few weeks it's just... I thought that was why I was late, cos it can affect you, stress. But then I thought, what if... Right...That should be long enough

SPIDER When you're wounded and left on Afghanistan's plains,
And the women come out to cut up what remains,
Jest roll to your rifle and blow out your brains
An' go to your Gawd like a soldier.
A soldier, a soldier, a soldier
An' go to your Gawd like a soldier.

VICKY Here goes...

LINDA Can't wait!

An explosion, far away.

SPIDER Yatesy!

Darren starts awake. Vicky gasps.

Linda turns as if hearing something.

VO It is with sadness that the Ministry of Defence must announce that a soldier from Thirty-four Regiment

Royal Engineers has been killed today in Afghanistan. The soldier was taking part in a foot patrol to disrupt insurgent freedom of movement and to reassure the local population when he was caught in the blast from an improvised explosive device. He was airlifted to the field hospital in Camp Bastion but was declared dead on arrival. A spokesman said the thoughts of all within Task Force Helmand are with his family and friends at this difficult time.

Scene Nine

Linda gets ready for the funeral as a military band plays 'Abide With Me'.

LINDA He was a beautiful baby. Well, obviously I would say that but it wasn't just me. We'd been trying for ages and when I finally got pregnant, John – oh, he was over the moon. It was a difficult labour. Long, you know, and when he finally came, he tore me quite badly. I didn't care. My word, could he cry! But to see him sleeping... Hold him... His skin against mine... And John's eyes, too: his dad's eyes...

It's funny – I don't mean funny but you know what I mean – cos you know from the day they join up, from the day they go over there, you know it's a possibility. Soldiers die sometimes. In every war there's ever been soldiers have died. So you think you'd be ready for it, wouldn't you?

I saw them as I turned the corner. Standing by the car, they were. It must be a terrible job. I hope it's not all they get to do.

A flag-draped coffin on which Chris's No 1 hat, medal, gloves and belt are laid. Linda and Vicky in black coats. Darren, in dress uniform, hands Linda the hat, medals, gloves and belt.

LINDA Thanks, Darren. Thanks, love.

She goes.

VICKY   Darren?

DARREN   Yeah.

VICKY   I'm pregnant.

DARREN   You sure?

Vicky nods.

DARREN   If it's a boy we're calling it Chris.

End of Act Two.

ACT THREE

Prelude

Chris folds the flag.

SPIDER 'Have you news of my boy Jack?'
Not this tide nor any tide.
'When d'you think that he'll come back?'
Not with this wind blowing...

'Has any one else had word of him?'
Not this tide nor any tide.
For what is sunk will hardly swim,
Not with this wind blowing...

'Oh, dear, what comfort can I find?'
None this tide nor any tide,
Except he did not shame his kind —
Not even with that wind blowing...

Then hold your head up all the more,
This tide, yes and every tide;
Because he was the son you bore,
And gave to that wind blowing...

Scene Ten

Linda in Christopher's room, reading sympathy cards / with a photo of Chris in uniform. Chris is there, unseen by Linda.

LINDA   People have been very kind. Some of the things they've said about him... Cards and that from some of the lads he served with. And they've written things – tributes like – on the Army site cos there's a page, you know, announcing his death. It's funny in a way, to hear him described like that: hero, legend! You think, Christopher? You should see him

127

when there's a spider in the bath.

CHRIS   Hey, don't go telling people stuff like that, I've got a reputation to preserve.

LINDA   But it's lovely to know he'll be missed. Remembered. *(Beat)* Darren hasn't really said anything. Not sure it's really sunk in. I mean obviously he knows – was there for heaven's sake, but he can't seem to find the words. Not sure I can. They were... Like brothers, really. Closer...

CHRIS   Double trouble...

LINDA   Of course the world doesn't stop turning. Life goes on. Everywhere you look, people are getting on with their lives – course they are – why wouldn't they? And you're getting on with things too. Getting up, going to work, shopping... But it doesn't mean anything... The weeks go by and the months go by but nothing means anything... When John died – my husband – it was a shock, you know, cos he was only in his thirties and you don't expect heart attacks at that age, do you? But there was Chris... I'd Chris to see to... Things still meant something. But now...

CHRIS   Come on...

LINDA   The other night, well, it was the middle of the night but anyway, I turned on the telly and it was *Zorba The Greek*, you know, the film with whats-is-name and the other one – English actor... was in that film with Omar Sherif – not Omar Sherif, Oliver Reed – oh, it's going to drive me mad if I can't... Anyway, it was half-way through or something and Zorba – Anthony Quinn!

CHRIS   Who?

LINDA   ... says to... the English bloke: *Why do the young die? Why does anybody die?* And the English bloke – he's a writer in the film - says: *I don't know.* And Anthony Quinn says: *What's the use of all your damn books? If they don't tell you that, what the hell do they tell you?* And the English bloke says: *They tell me of the agony of men who cannot* *answer questions such as yours. (Beat)* Alan Bates. That's who I mean.

CHRIS   Never heard of him.

LINDA   Alan Bates. He was handsome when he was young...

Vicky, now very pregnant, off- stage.

VICKY   Hello?

LINDA   Is that you, Vicky, love?

VICKY *(entering)* You left the back door open...

LINDA   Did I?

VICKY   I did knock... What you doing up here?

LINDA   Oh, you know... Just...Course it was never like this when... All over the place half the time: *Where's this? Can't find that! Mum, can you iron my shirt?*

CHRIS   Well, that's one thing the army taught me.

LINDA   Could iron a shirt better than me when he'd finished.

CHRIS   Yeah, well that wouldn't be difficult.

LINDA   Sometimes – you'll think I'm daft now – I mess the place up, pull the covers back on the bed, throw a few things on the floor as if... *(Beat)* Told you it was daft.

VICKY   No.

LINDA   All his things: T-shirts, trainers, smart shirts for going out... Some of this stuff's never been worn... He's never had these pants out of the packet.

CHRIS   And why would that be?

LINDA   I got them in a sale at BHS.

CHRIS   I rest my case.

LINDA   Proper trendy, I thought.

CHRIS   Well, you know what thought did.

LINDA   Course, one time underpants were just that: something you wore under your pants.

CHRIS   What *are* you talking about?

LINDA   Didn't matter what they looked like cos nobody saw them.

VICKY   Not now!

LINDA   No, these days it's all about having the right label.

CHRIS   Exactly.

LINDA   Cos half your backside's on display.

CHRIS   It's called –

LINDA   Fashion, I suppose.

CHRIS   Thank you.

VICKY   They're worse than girls half the time.

CHRIS   Don't you start!

LINDA   I thought they were nice.

CHRIS   Look, do you think you could talk about something other than my underpants.

Pause. Linda puts the pants away.

VICKY   Keep thinking about him...

LINDA   Yeah. *(Beat)* I never think of him... Like to think of him... as he was, you know... before...

VICKY   Come on.

LINDA   I used to love to see him – this sounds kinky but I don't mean it like that, but... If I ever saw him... after a bath or something, getting ready to go out... He had beautiful skin. Took after his dad like that...

CHRIS   Hey, come on... you'll have me at it.

VICKY   Don't.

CHRIS   And you're right. It does sound kinky.

LINDA   Bloody Taliban. They don't fight fair. They fight dirty. Nineteen. What were they doing letting him out there when he was just nineteen?

CHRIS   It was my job.

VICKY   Don't go over it.

CHRIS   Mum...

LINDA   It's like I can hear him sometimes.

CHRIS   Mum...

LINDA   Daft, I know...

CHRIS   Don't think about it.

LINDA *(beat)* Oh listen to me! Didn't come round to listen to me going on, did you?

VICKY   You're all right.

LINDA   So how's Darren?

VICKY   Oh, you know... Still saying how he should've been there.

LINDA   I'm glad he wasn't, they say the other lad'll never walk again.

VICKY   He doesn't see it like that. Feels he's let people down.

LINDA   I don't see how. He was ill, wasn't he? And back on patrol himself the next week when that poor Corporal got it.

VICKY   Wife and two kiddies he left.

LINDA   You wonder sometimes, what the bloody hell we're doing there in the first place.

VICKY   You know the answer to that.

LINDA   Some job!

VICKY   It's what they say.

CHRIS   Well, it is. And what other jobs were there?

LINDA   Still, with any luck you've got Darren home for a good while now.

VICKY   That's what we thought but apparently, they might be deploying them again next year.

LINDA   Oh, Vicky!

CHRIS   Shit...

LINDA   You won't have had the baby five minutes.

VICKY   I know.

LINDA   What does Darren say?

VICKY   Not a lot. Try to talk to him, he's off running.

LINDA   Running?

VICKY   It's all he does.

LINDA   You are all right, are you?

VICKY   Yeah, you know... Yeah.

LINDA *(with the flag)* Will you give him this? I thought he might... I don't know...

VICKY   Yeah.

SPIDER   Man down!

Darren wakes up, terrified.

Interlude

SPIDER   When I would muse in boyhood
                The wild green woods among,
                And nurse resolves and fancies

Because the world was young,
It was not foes to conquer,
Nor sweethearts to be kind,
But it was friends to die for
That I would seek and find.

I sought them far and found them,
The sure, the straight, the brave,
The hearts I lost my own to,
The souls I could not save.
They braced their belts about them,
They crossed in ships the sea,
They sought and found six feet of ground,
And there they died for me.

Darren has a knife. He's shaking.

Scene Eleven

Vicky nurses her baby.

VICKY   I was relieved in some ways cos it meant he wouldn't be going back, you know to Afghan, but then he was away when Gemma was born. Apparently, he lost it when this Corporal went off on one about his kit. Really went for him. Not like Darren that. Been drinking. That wasn't like him either but he got six months. Colchester. That's where they send them. I went to visit but he didn't want me taking Gemma... Not that she'd have known it was a prison. Then it was Dishonourable Discharge and off you go with forty quid in your pocket. So yesterday was the first time you got to see your daddy, wasn't it? *(Beat)* Not sure what we're going to do now though...

Darren enters in running gear.

VICKY   Good one?

DARREN   Yeah, you know... Got her off, then?

VICKY   Just wind, I think. One good burp and she was out like a light.

DARREN   All right for some.

VICKY   Yeah...

DARREN   About last night –

VICKY   It doesn't matter. To me, I mean.

DARREN   Well, it bloody matters to me.

VICKY   Keep your voice down. You'll have her awake.

DARREN   Spare me that!

VICKY   Darren!

DARREN   She never stops crying.

VICKY   She's a baby, Darren. Babies cry.

DARREN   Sorry, just... *(Beat)* I wanted to...

VICKY   I know. I know you did.

DARREN   Make love to you, be inside you – Christ, you don't know how much I've thought about it all these months.

VICKY   I know.

DARREN   So don't go telling me it doesn't matter.

VICKY   Probably just tired.

DARREN   Since when are you a medical expert?

VICKY   So go and see the doctor.

DARREN   And tell him what? I can't get it up any more? How's that make me look?

VICKY   He's not bothered! And you could talk about...

DARREN   What?

VICKY   ... How you're feeling and that.

DARREN   Not feeling anything.

VICKY   Is that right?

DARREN   And you'd know, would you?

VICKY   I know you were thrashing about last night, shouting in your sleep.

DARREN   Strange bed, that's all.

VICKY   You could ask him to give you something.

DARREN   Look, there's nothing bloody wrong with me, OK?

VICKY   OK. OK... (*Pause.*)

DARREN   Just tired...

VICKY   Yeah.

DARREN   So bloody tired... (*Pause.*)

VICKY   Here, take her, will you?

DARREN   Er...

VICKY   Come on, I want to take a picture!

DARREN   No, it's just...

VICKY   Look, you better get used to it! Here... That's right...

DARREN   I'm not sure...

VICKY   Aw!

DARREN   Vicky...

VICKY   What?

DARREN   I can't...

VICKY   What?

Flashback to image of Darren with dead child.

DARREN   No!

Darren thrusts the baby at Vicky and runs off to be sick.

VICKY   Darren!

Interlude

SPIDER Out of the night that covers me,
Black as the pit from pole to pole,
I thank whatever gods may be
For my unconquerable soul.

In the fell clutch of circumstance
I have not winced nor cried aloud.
Under the bludgeonings of chance
My head is bloody, but unbowed.

Beyond this place of wrath and tears
Looms but the Horror of the shade,
And yet the menace of the years
Finds and shall find me unafraid.

It matters not how strait the gate,
How charged with punishments the scroll,
I am the master of my fate:
I am the captain of my soul.

Darren shivers, shakes. Vicky can only look on.

Scene Twelve
Linda at home.

LINDA   Hello love!
VICKY   Hello.

LINDA   What brings you?

VICKY   Oh, you know...

LINDA   Everything all right?

VICKY   Yeah. Yeah...

LINDA   But not really.

VICKY *(beat)* I don't know what's happening.

LINDA   How d'you mean?

VICKY   With Darren.

LINDA   Have you had a row?

VICKY   That's all we do.

LINDA   Not like you two.

VICKY *(beat)* Not sure who he is anymore.

LINDA   What's brought this on?

VICKY   It started... *(Beat)* We're having trouble, you know...

LINDA *(beat)* A lot of men go through that.

VICKY   That's what I said. What's it matter anyhow? But then...

LINDA   What?

VICKY   He's so jumpy all the time. Look at him... he bites your head off. Put a cup down wrong, he's shouting. And as for Gemma... He just can't seem to... Then he's up half the night.

LINDA   Doing what?

VICKY   Running. Or drinking.

LINDA   How much?

VICKY   Too much but he won't have it. Says it helps him sleep.

LINDA   And does it?

VICKY   Sometimes. But then he has these dreams... Thrashing about, shouting. And he's wet through with sweat. Have to change the bed.

LINDA   He should go to the doctor's.

VICKY   He won't even talk about it.

LINDA   Oh, love. Has he seen his dad?

VICKY   No. *(Beat)* And there's something else.

LINDA *(beat)* Has he hit you?

VICKY   What? No! No, it's not that. But he scares me sometimes.

LINDA   Why?

VICKY   He's got a knife.

LINDA   What kind of –

VICKY   Great big thing. God knows where he got it. I found it under the bed. Says he needs to know it's there in case.

LINDA   In case what?

VICKY   He wouldn't say. He's got tablets too, paracetamol. Loads of them. In a box with the knife.

LINDA   How long has this been going on?

VICKY   Started after Chris died – no, before! When he was home on leave that time... I don't know... But since he's been back from Colchester...

LINDA   Why didn't you say?

VICKY   He didn't want people knowing. And you've had enough to cope with.

LINDA   Don't be daft.

VICKY   Then yesterday, we were in Asda and... someone must've dropped a bottle of wine or something – cos there was a hell of a bang – I mean I jumped and Gemma, well it set her off and you know what she can be like – but...

LINDA   What?

VICKY   When I looked round, he was on the floor, Darren. On the floor, shaking... sort of whimpering. And everyone looking. We just left the trolley and went home.

LINDA   Oh dear.

VICKY   And he'd wet himself.

LINDA   He needs to see a doctor.

VICKY   He just gets angry.

LINDA   Or will he come and see me, do you think? Do you think if I had a word...?

VICKY   I don't know. But I'm not sure how much more I can take.

Interlude

SPIDER   Bent double, like old beggars under sacks,
             Knock-kneed, coughing like hags, we cursed
             through sludge,
             Till on the haunting flares we turned our backs,
             And towards our distant rest began to trudge.
             Men marched asleep. Many had lost their boots,
             But limped on, blood-shod. All went lame;
             all blind;
             Drunk with fatigue; deaf even to the hoots
             Of tired, outstripped Five-Nines that dropped
             behind.
             Gas! GAS! Quick, boys! – An ecstasy of fumbling
             Fitting the clumsy helmets just in time,
             But someone still was yelling out and stumbling
             And flound'ring like a man in fire or lime...

Dim through the misty panes and thick green light,
As under a green sea, I saw him drowning.
In all my dreams before my helpless sight
He plunges at me, guttering, choking, drowning.
If in some smothering dreams you too could pace
Behind the wagon that we flung him in,
And watch the white eyes writhing in his face,
His hanging face, like a devil's sick of sin;
If you could hear, at every jolt, the blood
Come gargling from the froth-corrupted lungs,
Obscene as cancer, bitter as the cud
Of vile, incurable sores on innocent tongues, –
My friend, you would not tell with such high zest
To children ardent for some desperate glory,
The old Lie: *Dulce et decorum est*
Pro patria mori.

Darren drinking.

Scene Thirteen

Linda with a tent in a bag.

DARREN   Can I borrow it, then?

LINDA   Course you can, love. You can have it. It's very small though – you were only little when you slept in it.

DARREN   I know.

LINDA / SPIDER   Happy days, eh?

DARREN   Yeah.

LINDA *(beat)* Vicky said you've been running a lot.

DARREN   Yeah.

LINDA   Keeping fit?

DARREN Yeah. *(Pause)* I have these dreams.

LINDA She said.

DARREN No, not them. I do have them but I have these other ones, I couldn't tell her.

LINDA Do you want to tell me?

Pause.

DARREN It's the baby... in the dream. I've killed the baby.

LINDA But you haven't, love. She's fine. You'd never harm your Gemma.

DARREN No?

LINDA No.

DARREN There was that kiddie in Afghan.

LINDA That was an accident.

DARREN I go to check the casualties and there she is. I pick her up and she's like a rag – just like a rag.

LINDA You're getting all mixed up. It wasn't like that.

DARREN And other times we're back in basic training. On the range with the dummies.

LINDA Dummies?

DARREN Bayonet training.

SPIDER Fix bayonets!

CHRIS Yes, Corporal!

SPIDER Spirit of the bayonet!

CHRIS Kill, kill, kill!

SPIDER What makes the grass grow?

CHRIS Blood, blood, blood.

LINDA It's just a dream.

DARREN And you charge the dummy: screaming, stabbing.

LINDA   Darren, love, it's just a –

DARREN   And it's Chris, not a dummy anymore. Chris. I'm killing Chris.

LINDA   You weren't even there, love. You weren't even there that day.

DARREN   And why not?

LINDA   You were ill, you were ill – not even on duty.

DARREN   Should've been there.

LINDA   No.

DARREN   Should've been there and I wasn't.

LINDA   You were there the next time.

DARREN   Told you I'd look after him.

LINDA   And you did, I know you did.

DARREN   But I didn't, did I? Cos I'm alive and he's dead.

LINDA   Oh, Darren, love, you mustn't –

DARREN   But I promised you.

LINDA   It's not your –

DARREN   Promised.

LINDA   All right, love. It's all right... all right...

Pause.

DARREN   Every car backfiring, every Muslim bloke in the street... Sounds... Smells... And you're back there. And at night... Do anything to sleep... So you drink yourself unconscious but then the dreams come and you wake up soaking wet and screaming, lashing out...

LINDA   What about a doctor? They might be able to give you something.

DARREN   Saw one in Colchester. Anti-depressants so you feel like a zombie and sleeping pills so can't even wake up when you're having a nightmare. That was his big idea. No thanks.

LINDA   Well what about one of the service charities? I think there's one runs courses – therapy and that. Shall I ask at the Legion?

DARREN   If you like...

LINDA   It's just... I worry about you.

DARREN   Yeah

LINDA   And Vicky. You've had a rough time.

DARREN   Yeah.

LINDA   I just want... You won't do anything daft, will you?

DARREN   I don't know, that's it. I don't know anymore.

Interlude

SPIDER   What passing-bells for these who die as cattle?
– Only the monstrous anger of the guns.
Only the stuttering rifles' rapid rattle
Can patter out their hasty orisons.
No mockeries for them; no prayers nor bells,
Nor any voice of mourning save the choirs,
– The shrill, demented choirs of wailing shells;
And bugles calling for them from sad shires.
What candles may be held to speed them all?
Not in the hands of boys, but in their eyes
Shall shine the holy glimmers of goodbyes.
The pallor of girls' brows shall be their pall;
Their flowers the tenderness of patient minds,
And each slow dusk a drawing-down of blinds.

Scene Fourteen

In the garden. Darren in a sleeping bag.

VICKY   What you doing out here? *(Pause)* Darren, it's three o'clock in the morning.

DARREN   Yeah?

VICKY   Yeah. And bloody freezing.

DARREN   Is it?

VICKY   I woke up, thought you must have gone for a run but... what are you doing?

DARREN   Trying to get some fucking sleep.

VICKY   Right... Look, why don't you come back to bed?

DARREN   No.

VICKY   You can't be sleeping in the garden.

DARREN   Says who?

VICKY   What about the neighbours?

DARREN   Like I give a stuff.

VICKY   Darren!

DARREN   Leave it will you!

The baby cries. Darren freezes.

VICKY   Now look what you've done!

VOICE *(Off)* Do you know what time it is? If you don't knock it off, I'm calling the police.

VICKY   What did I tell you? *(Beat)* Darren..?

Darren has the knife, taken from a bag.

VICKY   Darren, put that down, you're frightening me now. *(But Darren is somewhere else...)* Darren... Darren!

SPIDER   Man down!

Image of Darren carrying Chris's body.

Darren stuffs the knife into the bag and runs off.

VICKY   Darren!

Interlude

Spider reads a newspaper.

VO   The body of a man believed to be an ex-soldier has been found in a wooded area close to the A22 near Downham. Police say the man died as the result of knife wounds which appear to have been self-inflicted.

Vicky with the baby.

LINDA   Please God, not him and all...

Scene Fifteen

Linda at home.
(Note: In the first production, the actor playing Spider took Darren's part up to his re-appearance in a towel after his shower).

DARREN   Hello, Mrs Yates.

LINDA *(beat)* Darren! Where have you...? When we heard about that lad who killed himself...

DARREN   Who's that?

LINDA   Doesn't matter... Months ago now.

DARREN   Right...

LINDA   So where've you been?

DARREN   Travelling, you know. Walking. Hitching lifts. Not that you get many of them when you start to stink.

And I must do. Not had a wash in weeks... longer. Same stinking shirt, pants... Made it to Wales, though. Cockle picking. Remember? Then I ended up near where me and Chris... near the barracks, you know. Not sure if I meant to end up there but that's where I ended up.

LINDA   Where were you sleeping?

DARREN   Can always find somewhere to sleep – army training for you, that. Needed to be in the open air. Hear the birds and that, smell the earth... Anyhow it must have been... there must've been a platoon passing out cos I noticed all the cars arriving – civilian cars, you know – and so I found a spot by the perimeter fence where you can just about see the parade ground and then I hear it: Durr-durr-dum! Durr-durr-dum!

And we can hear the band.

And the platoon comes marching round in strict parade formation – not one bastard out of step; not one step out of time – and all togged up and their families clapping and cheering and the lads trying not to smile – that's the hardest part of all – and the CO saying what a fine body of young men they are and all that shit the CO's say and the mums crying and the dads trying not to and everyone so proud. The proudest day of your life – to be a soldier in the British Army. And that was me. Me and Chris.

And Chris is there in his parade dress.

DARREN   And I'm watching them, having their photos taken and their girlfriends in shoes that are giving them gip and their little brothers trying their caps on and I'm crying – crying like a fucking baby – crying my eyes out and then this guard – doing his rounds with his dog, you know. And I knew him. Recognised him. And he tells me to piss off out of it. And I wanted to tell him it was me. But I couldn't. So I went. And now I'm here. Sorry. I must stink.

LINDA   Well, that's easily remedied. I'll run you a bath, shall I? Or a shower? Why don't you have a shower? A shower might be better... I've got one of them new boilers now. Hot water whenever you want.

DARREN   I'm not sure...

LINDA   What?

DARREN   I don't want to mess the place up.

LINDA   Don't be daft!

DARREN   And I get... Being enclosed like...

LINDA   Well, what if you keep the door open a bit?

DARREN   Could you stay outside – be outside like... talk and that, so I know you're there?

LINDA   If you like. I won't peek! Go on then. There's a clean towel on the rail. And there's some of Chris's shower gel, I think. Well, there is, yeah... You can use that. Go on.

He goes for a shower. Linda picks up his bag and comes across the book of poems.

DARREN   Are you there?

LINDA   Yes, love. I'm here. Just thinking, you know... Do you remember when you fell in the canal? You'd be ten...

CHRIS   Eleven.

LINDA   Ten or eleven. Been fishing I suppose – anyhow, it was one of your famous expeditions – and you must've had a row, I don't know, and Chris must've pushed you or something – fighting – but anyhow, you ended up in the canal and you turned up, like a drowned rat – soaked! – soaked to the skin and crying, trying not to cry but crying. And I don't know if you were more upset about having rowed or because you thought you'd be in trouble for getting your clothes wet – cos God knows what was in that canal - and we'd to get you in the bath, clean you off and into a pair of Chris's pyjamas while I washed your stuff and got it dry. Do you remember that?

CHRIS   Yeah...

LINDA   And we had hot chocolate and toast with whatsit.

CHRIS   *Nutella.*

LINDA   And I rang your dad to tell him you were staying over and Chris got into his pyjamas too and we ended up with the pair of you on the big sofa watching *Match of the Day* and Chris's dad went for fish and chips –

CHRIS   Chicken pie!

LINDA   But you had pies, the both of you, cos you didn't like the fish from our chippie, did you?

CHRIS   They leave the skin on!

LINDA   And we had shandy and then you both fell asleep so we just covered you with a duvet and left you there and in the morning, there you were, curled up like twins and the quarrel all forgotten. Tweedle-dum and Tweedle-dee.

DARREN *(re-appearing in a towel)* Double trouble.

LINDA   That's right...

DARREN   What is it?

LINDA   That shower gel... The smell...

DARREN   I thought you said to –

LINDA   No, I did. I did... Well, you look a bit more like your old self.

DARREN   Yeah.

LINDA   Here, do you want to give me your things and I'll put 'em through a wash while we have something to eat?

DARREN   Er..

LINDA   You might have to wear my dressing gown but they're unisex really these days. Just a bit small, maybe.

DARREN   No, I'm not... Not sure they're worth washing really... Bit of a mess.

LINDA   Right... that settles it. You can have some of

Chris's stuff –

DARREN   No.

LINDA   Well you've got to wear something! And it makes no sense them being in the wardrobe when you could be getting some use.

DARREN   What shall I do with...?

LINDA   I'll get a bin liner then, shall I?

DARREN   Yeah. Sorry.

LINDA *(going)* And then we'll get you something to eat.

DARREN   *Nutella* on toast?

LINDA *(off)* Oh, I think you could do with a bit more than that.

Darren shivers. He looks like a child.

LINDA *(entering with a pile of clothes and a bin liner)* Here. I think these are all new – not the trainers but they're not old... sweat shirt, tracksuit bottoms – I got them from the catalogue while he was away. And these pants – I bought these for him before you went the first time so why they're still in the packet, I don't know.

CHRIS   Bloody hell!

LINDA   I know they're not very trendy –

DARREN   No, they're fine. Honest.

LINDA   Right, you get dressed and I'll take these to the bin and then put the kettle on.

Linda takes the bin liner and goes. Darren gets dressed – in something like the clothes Spider wears now. Chris picks up the book.

SPIDER   The night is freezing fast,
Tomorrow comes December:
And winterfalls of old
Are with me from the past:
And chiefly I remember

How Dick would hate the cold.

Fall, winter, fall: for he,
Prompt hand and headpiece clever,
Has woven a winter robe,
And made of earth and sea
His overcoat for ever,
And wears the turning globe.

LINDA *(returning)* Are you decent?

DARREN   Yeah.

LINDA   Well, that's a bit better, isn't it? They fit all right?

DARREN   Just about.

LINDA   What's that you've got?

DARREN   It's –

LINDA   Oh, that's an old thing, I didn't mean to give you that. There is a jacket, one I bought him, hardly worn. Why don't I get you that?

DARREN   OK.

LINDA   And how about Vicky? Are you going to see her while you're here?

DARREN   I'm not sure she –

LINDA   No, she does. She will. And you should see your Gemma. What a smasher she is! Walking now! Talking soon!

DARREN   I've still got the knife...

LINDA   Right... Did you ever go on that course? With the charity?

DARREN   Got kicked off, didn't I? Drinking,

LINDA   Oh, well, never mind. Listen, I've been on the computer – get me, I know! – and there's other places you can go, other charities and that, people you can talk to –

DARREN   I'm not seeing any more doctors!

LINDA   No, not doctors – and nothing to do with the army, not officially, who might... you never know... be able to help. They say they can. They say they've helped some lads like you. That's what they say. I've printed it all off. If I get the details... Maybe you could give 'em a call... Shall I get them?

DARREN   If you like.

LINDA   And I'll get you that jacket and all.

She goes but when she comes back he's taken the old jacket and gone.

Interlude

VICKY   I suppose these decisions have to be made. You just wonder sometimes if they'd make them the same way if it was their sons going out there and coming back with no arms and legs or too scared to go to sleep without a knife under the pillow, grown men who jump at every sound or wet the bed or can't feel anything anymore. Perhaps I'm being unfair, but you wonder sometimes. I do.

LINDA   It's hard enough for some of them to come back at all. We train 'em that well, they've forgotten how *not* to be soldiers; how the rest of us live. The boys who come back with terrible injuries... At least we're getting better at not looking the other way. But the ones whose injuries are in their heads... Nothing to see, is there? No-one wants to know. And we can't wait for *them* to ask for help. We've trained them, haven't we? Trained them to keep a lid on it. I'm not saying that's a bad thing but we can't just walk away and leave them to it.

VICKY   They keep saying he has a drink problem. I keep asking why. They keep saying he has a drug habit. I keep asking why. They keep saying he's got a criminal record. I keep asking why. But they don't answer. And I don't know where he is. And I want him back.

LINDA   They say it can take years to come to the surface. That what we're seeing now is just the tip of the iceberg. Well, we'd better get our act together, that's all I can say. It's not just the army. I mean, it is the army – it's all the forces I expect – but it's the MOD, the government and in the end, I suppose, it's us. Cos what's being done's being done in our name and if we don't say *stop* then we're saying *go,* saying it's OK – and maybe it is, I don't know – but in any case, what I'm saying is that we're responsible. All of us. We have to realise there's a price to pay for going to war and if we won't pay it, we're condemning these boys to a fate worse than death – and I mean what I say when I say that – condemning them to a life... well, with no rest. And if we forget them – go on forgetting them – may we never sleep easy again. I'm sorry. That's just how I feel.

Scene Sixteen

Darren looking for a place to sleep.

SPIDER   Hey!

DARREN   Ah!

SPIDER   What d'you think you're doing?

DARREN   Sorry, mate, just after getting some sleep...

SPIDER   Well, get it somewhere else.

Darren picks up a book that Spider has dropped.

DARREN   Where d'you get this?

SPIDER   What's it to you?

DARREN   That's...

SPIDER   Ex-soldier, aren't I?

DARREN   What regiment?

SPIDER   Engineers.

DARREN   Where d'you serve?

SPIDER   Afghan, Gulf, Falklands, Belfast, Korea, Arnhem, Passendale... Ubique.

DARREN   Who *are* you?

SPIDER   27428947: Corporal: Mullins.
26943542: Sergeant: Archer.
543652: Captain: Broadbent...
29894797: Private: Webb *(Beat)* They call me Spider.

Pause.

DARREN   Is this how it ends?

SPIDER   Maybe. Depends, you know.

DARREN   On what?

SPIDER   This and that... Other people... Facing up to stuff... You... Finding help... Taking it...

DARREN   Not sure I can do it on my own.

SPIDER *(beat)* There's someone here. Say's he's a mate.

CHRIS   I bloody am. *(Beat)* Well? Say something, dickhead.

Pause.

DARREN   Forgive me, yeah? Forgive me.

CHRIS   What's to forgive?

DARREN   Say it!

CHRIS   OK. Forgiven.

DARREN   Still alive though, aren't I?

CHRIS   That's the hard bit. Over for me before the medics arrived. Never stops for you.

DARREN   Will it ever?

CHRIS   Dunno.

DARREN   What's the point of being dead if you don't know the bloody answers?

CHRIS   Sorry.

DARREN   I've got a knife and that.

CHRIS   Yeah...

DARREN   Just so tired.

CHRIS   I know.

DARREN   If only I could...

CHRIS   Here... *(And he wraps him in the flag.)* Rest.

DARREN   What about the dreams?

CHRIS   Dream the other one.

DARREN   What's that?

CHRIS   The one you had in Afghan... remember?

DARREN   Oh, yeah. Yeah...

CHRIS   You soft bastard...

Postlude

Beautiful music.

Chris, Linda, Vicky and finally Darren begin to move, to dance and finally, to fly...

Spider opens the poetry book.

SPIDER   Everyone suddenly burst out singing;
And I was filled with such delight
As prisoned birds must find in freedom
Winging wildly across the white
Orchards and dark green fields; on – on – and out
of sight.
Everyone's voice was suddenly lifted;

And beauty came like the setting sun:
My heart was shaken with tears; and horror
Drifted away ... O but Everyone
Was a bird; and the song was wordless; the singing
will never be done.

The music begins to fade.

ALL *(singing)* Let us sleep now...
Let us sleep now...
Let us sleep now...

SPIDER At the going down of the sun and in the morning,
we will remember them...

ALL Let us sleep.....

Lights down.

The End.

ENTERTAINING ANGELS

ENTERTAINING ANGELS

Entertaining Angels was commissioned by New Perspectives Theatre Company and first performed at Lakeside Arts Centre Thursday 2nd May, 2013.

For New Perspectives Theatre Company

Daniel Buckroyd   Artistic Director at the time of commissioning

Jack McNamara   Artistic Director at the time of production

CHARACTERS

Reverend Stephen Parr, a Church of England minister

Mel Parr, his wife

Sue Hunt, his church warden

Jack Soward, a village man

Kevin, a travelling man

Thanks: to all the people who gave their time to talk to me during the course of my research (Sue Rowe, Rev Canon Glyn Evans, Father Derek White, Philip Deuk, Father Stephen Underdown, Reverend Peter Owen Jones, Very Reverend Jonathan Meyrick, Reverend Doctor Andrew Manson-Brailsford, Father Peter Edwards, Father Felix Mascarenhas, Andrew Chevalier, Emma Wells, Reverend David & Pat Farey); the actors who workshopped the play in May 2012 (Kate Adams, Ava Hunt, John Walters, Chris Porter and Chris Hogben); Lawrence Evans, Heather Dunmore and Kitty Pandoliano for all their help, and Daniel Buckroyd, without whom...

PART ONE: ADVENT

One: First Sunday in Advent

A man walking; Jack tending his wife's grave; Mel making a herbal tea (rather than coffee) in the vicarage; Stephen facing his congregation (which includes Sue) in church.

STEPHEN 'Then the kingdom of heaven will be like ten virgins who took their lamps and went to meet the bridegroom. Five of them were foolish, and five were wise. For when the foolish took their lamps, they took no oil with them, but the wise took flasks of oil with their lamps. As the bridegroom was delayed, they all became drowsy and slept.'

MEL I met him when I started at World Aid. We were both in Campaigns. I know office romances are a no-no but it was the slightly sporty, slightly scruffy, sensitive combo... Fatal. Anhow, I moved to fundraising to make things easier and we got a flat. I knew he went to church and that – helped out at the youth club – football training; discos - but I never realised – not sure he did – how deep it went... So when he told me he wanted to train for the ministry well, it was a bit, you know... Blimey! We'd just got married; were planning to go travelling before we settled down, had kids... I said: Yes, of course: if that's what you want to do; need to do. Of course. Yes. You must do it...

STEPHEN But at midnight there was a cry, 'Here is the bridegroom! Come out to meet him.' Then all those virgins rose and trimmed their lamps. And the foolish said to the wise, 'Give us some of your oil, for our lamps are going out.' But the wise answered, saying, 'Since there will not be enough for us and for you, go rather to the dealers and buy for yourselves.' And while they were going to buy, the bridegroom came, and those who were ready went in with him to the marriage feast, and the door was shut.

SUE To be honest he was a bit of a compromise candidate. Of course we knew Father Derek would retire one day but it still came as a shock. And then during the interregnum... The least said about that the better. I said to her, I said: I want to come to church to meet my God, Jennifer, not Praise the Lord! And then, when Alex... Well, I could live without tambourines. And being lumped in wit Barton, Mayfield and Pound as a group ministry... well, it's not made things any easier.

STEPHEN   Afterward the other virgins came also, saying, 'Lord, lord, open to us.' But he answered, 'Truly, I say to you, I do not know you. Watch therefore, for you know neither the day nor the hour.' This is the Gospel of the Lord.

CONGREGATION   Praise to you, O Christ.

Stephen looks at his congregation...

STEPHEN   Advent – a time of penitence and anticipation when we take the time to look into our hearts and souls – acknowledging our failings and asking God and our neighbours to forgive us our sins – in preparation for the coming of Jesus, just as we might prepare and clean our homes in anticipation of the arrival of our friends and families at Christmas time.....

MEL   So we forgot about the travelling and put the idea of kids on hold while he was at theological college – I was supporting him anyhow – and then it was straight into his first job: curate in a pretty run-down city parish. But when I saw him all dressed up and standing there in church – cos I tried at first to show willing, you know: tow the party line - it was... Well, I know this sounds odd, but it was only then that it hit me; that I thought: bloody hell: that bloke's a vicar and I'm married to him, I'm... a vicar's wife. Christ.

STEPHEN   We don't want to be still rushing round with the Hoover on Christmas morning and wondering if we've got everything we need for lunch, we want to have finished the cleaning and done all the shopping so we can welcome our guests, just as the wise virgins thought ahead and were ready to welcome the bridegroom to the feast...

SUE What worries me about him is... Is it naivety? And I'm not sure his wife... I mean, I'm all in favour of women having careers but she has to commute and it means she can't really... give him the support she otherwise might. And she's not a big church-goer. You do see her sometimes but I've never felt jeans were appropriate wear for Holy Communion.

STEPHEN And just as at Christmas we want to be ready in our turn to welcome the infant Jesus into our world, we can take the idea of advent one stage further, by being always ready to welcome Christ into our hearts - for as the Gospel reminds us: we know neither the day nor the hour... In the name of the Father, Son and Holy Spirit.

Jack positions a gnome on his wife's grave and talks over the words of the creed.

STEPHEN We believe in one God

CONGREGATION The Father, the Almighty, maker of heaven and earth...

JACK There. What do you think to that? Smasher, in't he? I got him at that new garden centre on the Derby road.

CONGREGATION ... of all that is, seen and unseen. We believe in one Lord, Jesus Christ, the only Son of God, eternally begotten of the Father, God from God, Light from Light, true God from true God, begotten, not made, through him all things were made...

JACK Bernie Roberts took me over in his van. He was after some of that woodchip, you know for paths and that. Not for him: he's doing a job for some woman over Barton way.

CONGREGATION ... For us and for our salvation he came down from heaven, was incarnate from the Holy Spirit and the Virgin Mary and was made man...

JACK I didn't take Buster cos we were having a spot of lunch – they do soup and a roll, you know – and you've to leave them outside, tied to a rail if you've a dog. And you know what he's like if he thinks he's missing out. So I left him in the garden having a run about.

CONGREGATION   ... For our sake he was crucified under Pontius Pilate; he suffered death and was buried. On the third day he rose again in accordance with the Scriptures; he ascended into heaven and is seated at the right hand of the Father...

JACK   He was all in when I got back. Mind, so was I. He slept all afternoon. I'd've joined him but the soup kept repeating and I couldn't find a Rennie. I shan't have it again.

CONGREGATION   ... He will come again in glory to judge the living and the dead, and his kingdom will have no end. We believe in the Holy Spirit, the Lord, the giver of life, who proceeds from the Father and the Son, who with the Father and the Son is worshipped and glorified, who has spoken through the prophets...

JACK   Right. That's you looking all neat and tidy. I'll see you tomorrow, my lovely girl.

CONGREGATION   ...We believe in one holy catholic and apostolic Church. We acknowledge one baptism for the forgiveness of sins. We look for the resurrection of the dead, and the life of the world to come...

Jack kisses his hand and touches the grave.

CONGREGATION   Amen.

The man walking...

Two: The Vicarage

Mel eating toast. Stephen enters.

MEL   Is this bread from the village shop?

STEPHEN   Er…

MEL   Thought we were getting it from that new bakery.

STEPHEN   It's just people notice, you know?

MEL   Where we buy our bread?

STEPHEN   And if we always buy it from the same place it looks like favouritism.

MEL   It is. We favour nice bread because this stuff's disgusting. And please don't tell me man does not live by bread alone.

STEPHEN   Well, he doesn't.

MEL   No – well he wouldn't want to, not if it came from the village shop. You're back nice and early.

STEPHEN   Sue's locking up. And I didn't really preach. Not, you know…

MEL   You spent ages on that.

STEPHEN   I started but I just couldn't face it so I jumped to the end.

MEL   Oh dear. Do you want one of these?

STEPHEN   What is it?

MEL   Ginger and… something.

STEPHEN   I'll make some coffee.

MEL   Only if you let me smell it.

STEPHEN   You must be allowed the odd one.

MEL   God knows. It's supposed to help.

STEPHEN *(making his coffee)* Guess how many people were there?

MEL   Seven.

STEPHEN   How did you know?

MEL   Because we have this conversation every Sunday.

STEPHEN   Sorry.

MEL   No, it's all right. (*They kiss and share the toast.*)

STEPHEN   It isn't though, is it?

MEL   What?

STEPHEN   All right.

MEL   Well, it's a bit boring if you want to know.

STEPHEN   No, I mean – seven! That's the same number – more or less – since I took over.

MEL   At least it's not gone down.

STEPHEN   And when I managed to get a few new faces in by ringing the changes, the old guard voted with their feet.

MEL   Until normal service was resumed.

STEPHEN (*beat*) Very funny.

MEL   I thought so.

STEPHEN   And then this morning, I looked at them as I started speaking: Mrs Bentley with her endless worries about whatever's worrying her this week – the flowers or –

MEL   The litter in the churchyard?

STEPHEN   No, that was last week... the Frazers with their weirdly silent child.

MEL   The one with..?

STEPHEN   Yes. Mr Laycock... that woman whose name I can never remember and Sue looking... well, how she looks.

MEL   And how is the Lovely Sue?

STEPHEN   I looked at them and I thought: I can't stand here and tell you to love one another when I can't do it. Not this morning, anyhow. I mean what's the bloody point?

MEL   What have they done now?

STEPHEN   I don't mean them. I mean me. What's the point of me?

MEL   Oh dear, is it that bad?

STEPHEN   I don't *do* anything.

MEL   You never stop!

STEPHEN   But does anything I do *do* anything?

MEL   Course it does.

STEPHEN   Everything I've suggested, every idea I've had to shake things up a bit, attract families, make the place more welcoming –

MEL   Well, it could do with that.

STEPHEN   – everything's been squashed or undermined or met with a deafening wall of apathy.

MEL   Silence.

STEPHEN   What?

MEL   It's a wall of silence – a wave of apathy but a wall of silence.

STEPHEN   Silence then. And apathy. And if I hear anyone else say *That's not how Father Derek used to do it...*

MEL   It's a village.

STEPHEN   So?

MEL   So you've not been here long.

STEPHEN   A year!

MEL   That's not long in a village. A year? Pah!

STEPHEN   *That's not how we did things in Father Derek's day...*

MEL   Maybe you should talk to someone.

STEPHEN   Who?

MEL   I don't know: the Dean, or Archdeacon – whoever it is.

STEPHEN   And say what?

MEL That you're finding it all a bit... What you've just said.

STEPHEN And how would that look?

MEL Surely they must –

STEPHEN I've only been here a year –

MEL That's what I'm –

STEPHEN – they don't want to know you're losing the plot. They'd love to hear that – really inspire confidence!

MEL Only trying to help.

STEPHEN Well, you're not.

She pulls a face. He pours his coffee.

MEL It's not fair...

STEPHEN Have one.

MEL Get thee behind me, Satan!

STEPHEN Mm... Delicious!

MEL Do you think it's worth it?

STEPHEN The IVF?

MEL No! You!

STEPHEN How d'you mean?

MEL I mean if this is how it makes you feel.

STEPHEN Course it's bloody worth it!

MEL You were the one saying –

STEPHEN Course it is!

MEL Right. All right. As long as we're clear.

(The phone rings. Mel checks the display.)

It's the Lovely Sue.

STEPHEN She can leave a message.

We can hear Sue saying something about the graveyard...

STEPHEN   She was wondering what you'd like to do at the Christmas fair.

MEL   And you said..?

STEPHEN   That you'd have a think and be in touch...?

MEL   Stephen!

STEPHEN   You don't like it if I take decisions for you – you're always saying that.

MEL   Not this!

STEPHEN   What then?

MEL   I thought I made it clear – to you and the Lovely Sue – that my involvement last year was a strictly one-off affair based on the wholly erroneous assumption that as vicar's wife I'd be only too happy to run the white elephant stall.

STEPHEN   You did it so well.

MEL   No.

STEPHEN   And it's at a weekend.

MEL   Exactly: a weekend – I know that means nothing to you (a weekend: Ooh, spooky! What's that?) but for us mortals –

STEPHEN   Please?

MEL   No. It's not buy-one-get-one-free. I'm your wife not the magician's bloody assistant.

STEPHEN   It's just what they've been used to.

MEL   What, in Father Derek's day?

STEPHEN *(beat)* All right. Point taken.

MEL   Good.

STEPHEN   Will you think about it though?

MEL   Stephen!

STEPHEN   For me...

MEL   God... You are so annoying.

STEPHEN   I'll let you smell my coffee.

MEL *(doing so)* Mm... Oh! Gill called and I've got the name of that IVF bloke.

STEPHEN   The private one?

MEL   Vafakis... Something... Greek anyhow.

STEPHEN   Greek?

MEL   They're all Greek according to Gill.

STEPHEN   Did she say how much?

MEL   Well, it depends – anyway, that's not the point is it?

STEPHEN   No, I know – just wondering.

MEL   Five grand... Maybe more.

STEPHEN   Blimey.

MEL   We can probably just about do it.

STEPHEN   It'd better bloody work. *(Beat)* So what now?

MEL   I've got to phone and make an appointment.

STEPHEN   A Wednesday, yeah?

MEL   I don't see why it has to be your day off.

STEPHEN   You know what it's like coming up to Christmas.

MEL   Oh, I do! A vicar's work is never done.

STEPHEN   Thanks for the sympathy.

MEL   Well Wednesday's are a bugger for me. I've got team meetings, departmental feedback –

STEPHEN   Sorry.

MEL　　　You bloody should be. Right, I'm going for a bath with Kirsty Young.

STEPHEN　　Room for a small one?

MEL　　　Well, I would say yes but I think you'll find the Lovely Sue's expecting a call.

STEPHEN　　Do I have to?

MEL　　　'Fraid so. Or we'll have her round. And I can live without that today.

The man walking… stopping… walking…

Three: The Churchyard

Stephen and Sue by Mrs Soward's grave…

STEPHEN　　Well, it's unusual, I'll give you that.

SUE　　　Unusual? I think it's rather more than that, Stephen!

STEPHEN　　I'm not sure –

SUE　　　It's inappropriate. This is consecrated ground.

STEPHEN　　There is a cross as well.

SUE　　　I wasn't aware garden gnomes appeared in the gospels.

STEPHEN　　I think it might be the apocrypha.

SUE　　　It's not a joking matter.

STEPHEN　　No. Sorry. I can see that with it being next to –

SUE　　　That's got nothing to do with it. This is a special place for many people. A holy place.

STEPHEN　　Of course. But I'm not sure what you want me to –

SUE   I want you to have a word with him. I want you to tell him it's not on.

STEPHEN   How long has it been here?

SUE   I noticed it after Communion, yesterday.

STEPHEN   But it's not exactly doing any harm, is it?

SUE   It's a slippery slope. There are rules.

STEPHEN   Well, you know what they say about rules.

SUE   I know what some people say about them but it would never have happened in Father Derek's day, I can tell you that.

STEPHEN   No. Of course not. I'll have a word then. Next time I see him. And what was the other thing?

SUE   Oh, yes. The chairs. For the parish hall.

STEPHEN   Yes. Good news. Apparently, if we go in with Lepton and Pound we could all get a discount for a bulk purchase.

SUE   Buy the same chairs for both parish halls?

STEPHEN   I think that's what was suggested at the PCC.

SUE   But they'll be wanting blue.

STEPHEN   Will they?

SUE   They've always had blue in the past.

STEPHEN   And we haven't?

SUE   I really don't think blue would be a suitable colour for the chairs in our parish hall.

STEPHEN   No?

SUE   No.

STEPHEN   I hadn't really given it much thought.

SUE   Well, happily Mr Bailey and I have.

STEPHEN   So no blue chairs, then?

SUE   I don't think so.

STEPHEN   No. So –

SUE   And while we're on the subject of seating, I have to tell you, Stephen, that some people aren't happy.

STEPHEN   Really? With what?

SUE   The proposal.

STEPHEN   ...?

SUE   Your proposal.

STEPHEN   ...?

SUE   The church is a listed building.

STEPHEN   Yes...

SUE   A beautiful building.

STEPHEN   Yes...

SUE   And does beauty have no part in how we worship God?

STEPHEN   I'm not quite sure –

SUE   I'm talking about the pews, Stephen.

STEPHEN   Ah.

SUE   The carpeted family area.

STEPHEN   I'm just trying to make the church – the church building – the Church – more... welcoming to a wider range of people... children... Just to see if it makes a difference.

SUE   We went through this with the service changes.

STEPHEN   It's just a proposal.

SUE   Well, it was never like this –

STEPHEN   Sue, the parish has to understand that I'm not Father Derek and I'm never going to be Father Derek and although I'm sure Father Derek was a lovely man, if anyone else so much as mentions Father Derek's name to me,

I swear I'll scream.

SUE   Well, I'm sure there'll be no need for that. But the pews have always been there.

STEPHEN   Well, that's just it, you see, they haven't.

SUE   Well, they've been there as long as anyone can remember.

STEPHEN   Maybe but until the 19th century there were no pews. Not in the nave. The congregation stood.

SUE   Well, that, Stephen, is what some people would call progress. And we wouldn't want to be anti-progressive, would we? And now here's Mr Soward so I'll leave you to have a word.

Sue goes as Mr Soward enters…

STEPHEN   Mr Soward.

JACK   Vicar.

STEPHEN   Stephen.

JACK   Aye.

STEPHEN   I was just… Your wife's grave…

JACK   Ellen.

STEPHEN   Yes. You've been making a few changes I see.

JACK   Oh, you mean..? Aye, I got him the other day.

STEPHEN   Right…

JACK   Been on the look out for ages – you know, for the right one. I mean I've plenty in the garden – you'll have seen the garden –

STEPHEN   Yes. Yes.

JACK   But I didn't want to bring any old one along. It wouldn't seem right, would it, with it being the churchyard?

STEPHEN   No. No, I can see that.

JACK   She had a bit of a thing for them, Ellen.

STEPHEN   Right…

JACK   Had them here, there and everywhere – even where you least expect.

STEPHEN   Yes.

JACK   We've ones from all over the country.

STEPHEN   Really?

JACK   And abroad – when we went abroad – the one with the sombrero –

STEPHEN   I don't think…

JACK   No, you won't have seen him, he's in the back, looking after the onions.

STEPHEN   Right…

JACK   With him being Spanish.

STEPHEN   Right…

JACK   That's what she liked to think, you see, that they were looking after things: standing guard, like.

STEPHEN   Right…

JACK   So when I saw this little feller, I knew he was the one to keep an eye on my lovely girl till I join her.

STEPHEN   Right… Of course Christ is here, too.

JACK   Oh, I'm not saying that. But you can't expect him to be on duty twenty-four seven, can you? I mean he's all these others to be watching out for.

STEPHEN   Yes. I expect he's got his hands full.

JACK   It's all right, then?

STEPHEN   I don't see why not.

JACK   Only some people can be a bit…

STEPHEN   Really?

JACK   I mean the last vicar –

STEPHEN   Father Derek –

JACK   He could be a bit, you know – looking down his nose.

STEPHEN   Really?

JACK   And then we had a woman while you got here. She caused a stink.

STEPHEN   I know some people still struggle with idea of women clergy.

JACK   Oh, I don't think anyone minded that, but she was one of them, you know...

STEPHEN   Really?

JACK   Oh, aye!

STEPHEN   I didn't know.

JACK   Always knocking on your ruddy door.

STEPHEN   What?

JACK   Evangelicals.

STEPHEN   Oh, I thought you meant...

JACK   What?

STEPHEN   It doesn't matter.

JACK   People don't want that.

STEPHEN   No?

JACK   Oh, they don't mind the odd visit but not when there's an agenda if you get my drift.

STEPHEN   Right...

JACK   It's a private thing, in't it? What you believe and don't believe or if you go to church or not.

STEPHEN   I wouldn't mind seeing a few more faces on a Sunday morning.

JACK   You'd've always seen my Ellen.

STEPHEN   I'm sorry I never met her.

JACK   She was a good 'un. Forty-three years.

STEPHEN   And never a cross word?

JACK   Oh, I wouldn't say that! She could take on, Ellen, if she didn't like something. But she never missed church of a Sunday.

STEPHEN   Did you ever go with her?

JACK   Christmas and that, you know. Church was always full then.

STEPHEN   Oh yes, Christmas, Easter, Harvest Festival.

JACK   There you are then.

STEPHEN   I suppose... Well, better get on. Have to see a man about a gutter.

JACK   Where's that then?

STEPHEN   Downham.

JACK   Are you in charge there, too?

STEPHEN   Five parishes now.

JACK   They get their money's worth, don't they!

STEPHEN   You could say that.

JACK   And what's the trouble?

STEPHEN   Every vicar's worst enemy: damp!

JACK   Thought it was the devil.

STEPHEN   Oh, the devil's nothing to a blocked down-spout.

JACK   Let's hope that's all it is.

STEPHEN   Yes, fingers crossed.

JACK   I'll say a prayer!

STEPHEN   Even better.

JACK   Cheerio then, Vicar.

STEPHEN   Stephen.

JACK   Aye.

Four: Thoughts and prayers

Mel sorting a pile of paperwork and Stephen in church.

MEL   I work from home one day a week. The commute's
a pain in the bum but you can't rely on the broadband here
half the time. And as the house goes with the job – Stephen's
job, that is – and as the parishioners – or so they tell themselves – pay for the job, they seem to think they can pop
round whenever they like, or telephone, day or night, about
anything and everything from graffiti on the bus shelter to
the state of the roads.

STEPHEN   I don't expect the Blessed Derek ever felt like
this. Twenty years and just the two parishes: a sort of cross
between George Herbert, Alistair Simm and Bagpuss. But for
all his saintliness, it seems to me Derek was happy to muddle
along. And I can't help wanting to stir things up a bit. I'm not
asking for the earth to move, I just want to help the people
of these parishes to come to You – to feel, to know, to share
Your love.

MEL   Most people don't want to know though. Not
really. Oh, they like seeing him about, having him at their
fetes and suppers but they don't want to get too involved.
Weddings, Christenings, funerals. Christmas, Easter,
Harvest Festival. That's about it.

STEPHEN   Sometimes... I won't say despair, I don't despair
but... This can't be why You came down to earth and died
for us, can it? This can't be the culmination of two thousand
years of persecution and great art and holy wars, the burning
question of whether or not to remove a couple of pews and

the colour of chairs in the parish hall?

MEL　　　I'm not criticising. I don't really get it either. Not really. Why it's so important. But to him it's central. And his failure to get the rest of us on board... It wears him down. Which is why I feel guilty. Because I resent it.

STEPHEN　　I'd talk to Mel but I've asked so much of her over the years. She's given up so much to let me do this because I told her this was what I had to do. You don't like to say you might have got it wrong, made a mistake. And all the sacrifices she's made, all the looks of disapproval she's had to put up with – that they might all have been for nothing. So you say nothing and hope for the best.

MEL　　　It's like he's having an affair – oh, not with another woman (that would be easy) no, with the whole parish and his need to follow God. But I need him too. I don't think he sees that sometimes but I do.

STEPHEN　　And I can't help wondering sometimes: what's the point? Not of You. Never of You. No. Of me. As a priest. As a husband. Of anything I do. Are You listening to this, Lord? Are You? Then give me something I can do. Just give me one single sodding thing I can actually do.

Five: The Church

This follows the last scene without a break. Kevin – the walking man – is there, perhaps lit from behind by the light from a stained glass window. Like he has a halo.

KEVIN　　　You couldn't... You wouldn't have something to eat, would you? A sandwich... Anything really. And a drink... I don't mean... cup of tea, you know... don't mean to be any trouble. But I've not eaten since yesterday... It doesn't have to be a sandwich, just some bread and cheese. Or bread. Just bread'd do. Bread and water.

Pause.

STEPHEN   Sorry, I didn't see you... Didn't hear you come in.

KEVIN   Is it all right?

STEPHEN   Yes.

KEVIN thought –   Only I saw the church across the fields. And I

STEPHEN   Yes. I just didn't hear you.

KEVIN   Sorry.

STEPHEN   No. No... Have you come far?

KEVIN   Just travelling, you know.

STEPHEN   Right.

KEVIN   On the road, like. Just travelling.

STEPHEN   Right. I thought about it one time... I don't mean... I mean abroad... With my wife when we first got married but...

KEVIN   Something came up.

STEPHEN   Yeah.

KEVIN   Stuff happens.

STEPHEN   Yeah.

KEVIN   And now you're a vicar.

STEPHEN   Yeah...

KEVIN *(after a pause)* Beautiful church.

STEPHEN   Yes. Yes, it is.

KEVIN   Peaceful.

STEPHEN   Yes.

KEVIN   Quiet.

STEPHEN   Yes. A bit too quiet sometimes.

KEVIN Don't you like it quiet?

STEPHEN No, it's just... No, quiet can be good.

KEVIN Takes a bit of looking after, I should think.

STEPHEN Just a bit.

KEVIN Maintenance.

STEPHEN I've another four.

KEVIN Churches?

STEPHEN Yes!

KEVIN Are there that many people wanting to come?

STEPHEN No, but they all want to come to *their* church.

KEVIN Busy, busy then.

STEPHEN You could say that. Course taken one at a time, things aren't so bad but you can't take them one at a time because they come along in twos and threes and everyone's got an opinion about how things should be done and even if they don't say anything to your face – which wouldn't be polite, would it? – they say it behind your back – which apparently is quite acceptable. And what's right for one parish is never right for another and when you've got five – well, you do the maths. But it doesn't stop you feeling guilty; like you're getting it wrong, letting them down because, let's face it, as far as they're concerned, you are. Some people try to help. Some are even helpful. But you're the man: the vicar, their vicar. And you're a big disappointment.

Pause.

KEVIN Right.

STEPHEN Sorry. *(He laughs)* You didn't really need to know all that, did you?

KEVIN Maybe you needed to get it off your chest.

STEPHEN Yes...

Pause.

KEVIN   What were you doing?

STEPHEN   When?

KEVIN   When I come in?

STEPHEN   I was, er... Praying. I was just praying.

KEVIN   What for?

STEPHEN   Not really for... Well... Talking to God, you know.

KEVIN   And was He listening?

STEPHEN   That's a good question.

KEVIN   Did He have anything to say?

STEPHEN   And that's another one.

KEVIN   Oh, I'm full of them.

STEPHEN   Nothing wrong with that.

KEVIN   Seek and ye shall find.

STEPHEN   Knock and it shall be opened unto you.

KEVIN   What man is there of you, whom if his son ask bread, will he give him a stone?

STEPHEN   Matthew, chapter seven.

KEVIN   I was an hungred, and ye gave me meat; I was thirsty, and ye gave me drink; I was a stranger and ye took me in. *(Beat. Stephen laughs nervously.)* Matthew, twenty-five.

STEPHEN   You know your Gospels then.

KEVIN   I like to read. But...

STEPHEN   You also like to eat.

KEVIN   Just something. Anything. And if I could doss for the night.

STEPHEN   Here?

KEVIN	Would that be all right?
STEPHEN	Look, why don't you –?
KEVIN	Do you want me to wait outside?

STEPHEN *(beat)* No. No, stay where you are. I'll just pop over the vicarage, see what I can do. Won't be long.

Stephen starts to go...

KEVIN	I'll just wait here then.

Stephen turns back.

KEVIN	Might have a word. You know.
STEPHEN	Yes... Yes.

Stephen goes. Kevin lies down.

Six: The Vicarage

Again following without a break.

MEL	No!
STEPHEN	He isn't a tramp or anything.
MEL	Oh, well then, bring him over!
STEPHEN	Really?
MEL	No!
STEPHEN	He doesn't have to eat with us.
MEL	That's right.
STEPHEN	And he could sleep in the study if you'd rather he wasn't upstairs.
MEL	Stephen, no.
STEPHEN	It would only be for a night. Couple of nights at most.

MEL   We never do this, you know that. It's not th
  we do it.

STEPHEN   I know, I just thought…

MEL   What?

STEPHEN   I don't know, he seems…

MEL   What? What do you know about him?

STEPHEN   Nothing.

MEL   Exactly. He could be ill – mentally ill.

STEPHEN   I don't think so.

MEL   But we don't know.

STEPHEN   No, all right.

MEL *(beat)*   This is you all over.

STEPHEN   What?

MEL   Lame ducks – they bring out the Mother Teresa
  in you.

STEPHEN   Is that so bad?

MEL   You can't just do things because it makes you feel
  better.

STEPHEN   I don't! *(Beat)* And what if I did? Would it matter
if it made him feel better too?

MEL   And what about me? How it'd make me feel?

STEPHEN   Why should it make you feel anything?

MEL   Because it's my house and he's a strange bloke.

STEPHEN   Nothing strange about him.

MEL   You know what I mean.

STEPHEN   He's actually quite interesting.

MEL   It would make me feel uncomfortable.

STEPHEN   I don't see why.

MEL *(beat)*   Did he ask if he could come to the house?

STEPHEN   No.

MEL   No. I expect if he'd wanted to, he'd've come here in the first place.

STEPHEN   He said he saw the church.

MEL   Which is where he went.

STEPHEN   So?

MEL   So I suggest you take him over some food and let him get on with it.

STEPHEN   There were complaints when we let that other bloke stay.

MEL   Well he did piss in the font.

STEPHEN   This bloke's not like that.

MEL   There you are then.

STEPHEN   But you know what people are like.

MEL   The Lovely Sue.

STEPHEN   Not just Sue. And it's cold.

MEL   So take him a blanket.

STEPHEN   Will that be enough?

MEL   I don't know. I expect so. Yes.

STEPHEN   Yeah. *(Beat)* Yeah. I'll make him a sandwich.

MEL   No, you put the kettle on – do a flask. I'll make the sandwich. God!

Seven: The Church

Sue confronts Kevin.

SUE   Well, you can't stay here, I'm afraid.

KEVIN   The vicar's just gone to get me some food.

SUE   Really?

KEVIN   The crumbs which fell from the rich man's table.

SUE   Well, if I could ask you to wait in the porch.

KEVIN   Because there was no room for them at the inn.

SUE   We've had trouble in the past, that's all, and as church warden it's my responsibility so if you wouldn't mind –

KEVIN   Though I speak with the tongues of men and of angels and have not charity, I am become as sounding brass or a tinkling symbol.

SUE   Very good.

KEVIN   Ye blind guides, which strain at a gnat, and swallow a camel.

SUE   I beg your pardon?

KEVIN   Ye are like unto whited sepulchres, which indeed appear beautiful outward, but are within full of dead men's bones, and of all uncleanness.

SUE   You needn't think you can frighten me.

KEVIN   There is no fear in love. But perfect love casteth out fear.

SUE   Yes, thank you.

KEVIN   He that loveth not, knoweth not God; for God is love.

SUE   I think we'll leave God out of this, shall we?

KEVIN   The foxes have holes, and the birds of the air have nests; but the Son of man hath not where to lay his head.

SUE   I'll ask you once more. Will you please leave the church?

KEVIN   Cast him into outer darkness; where shall be

weeping and gnashing of teeth.

SUE   I'm just asking you to wait in the porch.

KEVIN   Whatever you say. *(Beat)* Blessed is he that considereth the poor: the Lord will deliver him in time of trouble.

SUE   I'll remember that.

STEPHEN *(entering with food)* Oh, Sue! I see you've met...

KEVIN   My name is Legion: for we are many.

SUE   For heaven's sake!

KEVIN   Kevin. My name's Kevin.

STEPHEN   Right. I see you've met Kevin.

SUE   Yes.

STEPHEN   I was just getting some food.

SUE   And bedding.

STEPHEN   Yes.

SUE *(beat)* I'll leave you to it.

STEPHEN   Yes. Goodnight, Sue.

KEVIN   God Bless...

Beat. She goes. Pause.

STEPHEN   That was Sue.

KEVIN   Yes.

STEPHEN   Church warden.

KEVIN   She said.

STEPHEN   Yes. She worries sometimes... Only doing her job really.

KEVIN   I expect she'll be all right.

STEPHEN   Yes, well... My wife made the sandwiches. I did wonder if you should stay at the vicarage but she thought it might be best –

KEVIN   And I can see her point – she's quite right...

STEPHEN   So I've brought you some...

KEVIN   Thank you.

STEPHEN   My wife's not keen on that bread but I think it's fine. But what do I know? And there's tea in the flask. I put sugar in. I hope that's right.

KEVIN   Thank you.

STEPHEN   And a pillow and a blanket – in case you need it.

KEVIN   Thank you. You going to join me?

STEPHEN   Well, I can stay for a while.

Kevin takes a sandwich, breaks it and holds some out to Stephen. Pause.

KEVIN   What is it? Don't you want any?

STEPHEN *(beat)* No... No, You eat it.

KEVIN   Please yourself.

STEPHEN   I'll just...

KEVIN   Oh, right.

STEPHEN   Er... Thank you, Lord, for looking out for Kevin and bringing him to Your door so we could offer him some food and a place to rest in the spirit of love which Your son taught us. Amen.

KEVIN   Amen.

Kevin eats...

STEPHEN   You were hungry, then!

KEVIN   I was, yeah. *(Pause.)*
(*Singing*) My song is love unknown,
My Saviour's love to me;
Love to the loveless shown, That they might

lovely be.

O who am I, that for my sake My Lord should take, frail flesh and die?

STEPHEN   That's an old one!

KEVIN   I like the way it wanders about. Sometimes, when you're on the road, a song can keep you company. And it's nice to have a bit of company sometimes.

STEPHEN   Yes. *(He laughs.)*

KEVIN   What?

STEPHEN   Nothing, just... Sometimes I'll do morning prayers, or evensong... and there'll be no-one here. Not a soul. Just me.

KEVIN   What about God?

STEPHEN   Quite right. I was forgetting God.

KEVIN   Is He here now, do you think?

STEPHEN   I expect so.

KEVIN   In the giving, perhaps. In the bread. *(Beat)* Are you sure you don't want any?

STEPHEN   I'll get something later.

KEVIN   With your wife.

STEPHEN   Yes.

KEVIN   What does she think to your being a vicar?

STEPHEN   Oh, you know... I think it's hard on her sometimes.

KEVIN   Like being in the Forces.

STEPHEN   Is that what –?

KEVIN   Onward, Christian soldiers!

STEPHEN   Yes.

KEVIN   Any kids?

STEPHEN   No. No, not so far...

KEVIN   Oh well, you never know.

STEPHEN   No. Well, I'd better…

KEVIN   Course you had.

STEPHEN   Will you be all right, do you think?

KEVIN   Snug as a bug.

STEPHEN   If you need the loo… it's through the vestry.

KEVIN   Right.

STEPHEN   Last time… We had someone else stay… He used the font.

KEVIN   I wouldn't do that.

STEPHEN   No. No, I knew you wouldn't.

Eight: Sue

Sue walking her dogs; throwing balls for them to fetch. Perhaps we can hear children playing in the school.

SUE   There you go!

Father Derek had absolute rules about such things. When the issue arose he would call the police or social services. This is a village. We don't have the facilities. To say nothing of the risks. There's the school to consider.

Oh, Dixie, never mind! Is he too fast for you, these days?

Of course we have a duty to help those less fortunate than ourselves – I'm not saying that… that's part of what being a Christian is all about – but you'll have to forgive me if I choose to love my neighbour at one remove.

Leave. Good boy! Good boy, Leo!

This isn't the first time and, if I know Stephen, it won't be the last. And word will spread. You see if I'm wrong. We just don't have the facilities. I know he means well. I know he does. But you have to know where to draw the line.

Come on you two...

Nine: The Graveyard

Jack tending his wife's grave. Kevin is there, watching him. Jack sits and drinks tea from a flask. He sees Kevin.

JACK	Hello there.
KEVIN	Hello.

JACK *(after a pause)* Cup o' tea?

KEVIN	Can you spare it?
JACK	Oh, I've plenty. I drink too much.

Kevin joins him. Jack pours his tea.

JACK	Passing through?
KEVIN	On the road, you know.
JACK	Ex-Forces?
KEVIN	Fighting the good fight!
JACK	Aye. (*Giving him the tea)* There you go.
KEVIN	Thank you.

JACK *(after a time)* I was in Aden. Just six months, like. National Service. Cyprus first – that wasn't too bad. But I saw a few things, you know. Mind, I doubt it's anything to what you boys came across. *(Beat)* Young Alex here... that was terrible.

KEVIN *(reading)* Captain Alexander Hunt.

JACK He used to come round as a lad, play wi' Buster when he was a puppy. Or sometimes – Ellen didn't approve of this – he liked to see... I've a pistol – officer's pistol really so I should never've had it in the first place let alone kept it – from when I was in Aden. He liked to look at it, help me clean, sort of thing. Still got it in the shed. Hidden away like... *(Beat)* You don't see his dad now. Took it bad. But his mother's very involved with the church. A bit, you know... *(Beat)* How's your tea? Is it all right?

KEVIN   Yes. Thank you.

JACK   Not often you see anyone here in the week.

KEVIN   Peaceful.

JACK   Yes.

KEVIN   And you look after it, do you?

JACK   Just tidy up a bit. When my wife was buried, well... I thought the place looked a bit shabby, like it could do with a bit of attention. And I've always been fond of gardening, not vegetables so much, but flowers, you know... so I just sort of appointed myself and no one seems to object.

KEVIN   Probably grateful.

JACK   Oh, I don't know about that but the vicar's given me the thumbs up.

KEVIN   I met him last night. He seems decent enough.

JACK   Yes, he's all right, this one.

KEVIN   Let me sleep in the church.

JACK   Oh well, why not? I don't really know him. He always says hello, has a word. His wife too, sometimes. She works.

KEVIN   Right.

JACK   I'm not much of a church-goer myself. I mean my mother, she was Chapel and no messing and Ellen – my wife – she came regular but I've never... Just not my thing. Although I can tell you quite a bit about the history of the place. If you're interested. *(Beat)* Of course a lot of people aren't. *(Pause)* Yes, you'll find me here most days – if only to bring some flowers.

KEVIN   How long since she died, your wife?

JACK   Two years. In May...

KEVIN   What was she like?

JACK   Oh, she was... Always very smart, you know... Kept the house beautiful. And her eyes... first thing I noticed – violet. Like Elizabeth Taylor – not that she looked liked Elizabeth Taylor. But then I'm no Richard Burton.

KEVIN   I think I might've met her.

JACK   When?

KEVIN   Couple of years back – more – I was passing this way and I asked if she could spare me anything to eat. And she brought me out some... What was it now?

JACK   Shepherd's pie?

KEVIN   I think it might've been.

JACK   Was it in a dish?

KEVIN   Yes.

JACK   Blue and white?

KEVIN   That was it.

JACK   That's right. That's Ellen all over... *(Pause)* Still got that dish.

KEVIN   You must miss her.

JACK   It's funny the things you do miss. I can never get the cupboard door closed properly. Under the sink. She had a knack. And she'd hum – you know as she was doing... whatever she was doing. I miss that. The silence sometimes... And Buster... I think he misses her more than I do. Sits by her chair to this day. Like he's waiting, you know.

KEVIN   Good to have some company.

JACK   And he keeps me fit – going for a walk. Although he's got a bit of a cough at the moment so I'm keeping him in. *(Beat)* What did I tell you?

KEVIN   What?

JACK   Now I need to spend a penny.

KEVIN   There's one in the church.

JACK   Oh, I'll go behind the shed at the back. I've done it before. There's a compost heap. It's very good for it apparently. Helps it on, you know. Course you've to be careful. Don't want to frighten the horses.

KEVIN   I'll keep a look out.

JACK   Would you?

KEVIN   Give a whistle.

JACK   ...?

KEVIN   If anyone's coming.

JACK   Oh, aye!

Ten: The Vicarage

MEL   Has anyone said anything to you about our front garden?

STEPHEN   No. Why?

MEL   Apparently, the lawn is causing concern.

STEPHEN   Who to?

MEL   The Lovely Sue rang... this isn't her, of course, she was just passing on what she'd heard.

STEPHEN   Which was?

MEL   That people think it makes the village look untidy.

STEPHEN   Is it that bad?

MEL   Not really. Sort of a wildflower meadow, I thought.

STEPHEN   I've just got so much on at the minute.

MEL   Oh, she's aware of that, said more than once how we – *we* – couldn't expect you to be gardening on top of everything else.

STEPHEN   Then why was she calling?

MEL   Why indeed?

STEPHEN   ... No!

MEL   It's like that time she asked if I thought you were getting enough to eat, do you remember? I'm surprised she didn't want to know if I was washing your underpants properly.

STEPHEN   Actually, I've been meaning to talk to you about that –

MEL   Don't even joke about it.

STEPHEN   So what did you tell her?

MEL   I said it was up to you what you ate.

STEPHEN   About the lawn.

MEL   Oh, I said we were thinking of getting a goat.

STEPHEN   You didn't!

MEL   I should've done.

STEPHEN   But –

MEL   Can you imagine what that lot next door would say? Be worth it just to see their faces. *A goat! In the countryside! Whatever next?*

STEPHEN   But what you actually said was...?

MEL   I told her I'd see to it at the weekend.

STEPHEN   Ah...

MEL   What?

STEPHEN   It's Markham Autumn Fun Day this Saturday.

MEL   And?

STEPHEN   It's just... the PCC were very keen, you know... They wanted you to judge the displays.

MEL   And you said..?

STEPHEN   ... you'd be happy to?

MEL   Well, then, a goat it is!

STEPHEN   I didn't know how to say no.

MEL   Really? You say it to me all the time.

STEPHEN   That's not fair.

MEL *(beat)* I just wish you'd ask me sometimes.

STEPHEN   I'm sorry. It was just such a lousy meeting with them last time – Mr Reynolds going on and on about the need to replace the boiler and how that was somehow my fault and nothing I said could make him happy or even shut up –

MEL   So you thought a small sacrificial lamb might keep the wolves quiet for a bit.

STEPHEN   Sorry.

MEL   Just call me Agnes.

STEPHEN   Really sorry.

MEL   Oh, and talking of old boilers, that woman with the hair – you know *(She makes a gesture.)* – Brown Owl or whatever she is – flagged me down yesterday.

STEPHEN   Not still going on about –?

MEL   I'm just the messenger. No shooting, please.

STEPHEN   You'd think I'd tap danced on the graves of our glorious dead.

MEL   Well, I'd've thought any fool knew the Guides came before the Scouts when it comes to wreath laying. Perfectly obvious when you think about it.

The doorbell rings.

STEPHEN   Oh no! Who's this? I've got a wedding rehearsal in half an hour over at Downham

MEL   Oh, it'll be the Lovely Sue.

STEPHEN   You didn't say she was coming round.

MEL   Didn't I? Must have slipped my mind. Oh! It's going to be next Wednesday by the way.

STEPHEN   What is?

MEL   The appointment with Dr Vafakis.

STEPHEN   Wednesday?

MEL   Your day off.

STEPHEN   I know!

MEL   So don't go arranging anything.

The doorbell again.

MEL   I'll let her in, shall I?

Mel goes. Stephen steels himself.

MEL *(off)*   Hello, Sue.

SUE *(off)*   Melanie. Is Stephen...?

MEL *(off)*   In the kitchen, just go through. *(Beat)* There's tea in the pot. Help yourself.

Sue enters.

STEPHEN   Sue.

SUE   Stephen.

STEPHEN   Can I get you...?

SUE   No thank you.

STEPHEN   If this is about the lawn...

SUE   What? Oh, no – I spoke to Melanie about that. She's assured me it'll be sorted at the weekend.

STEPHEN   Right. *(Beat)* And I did have a word with Mr Soward about his wife's grave –

SUE   But to no effect.

STEPHEN   No.

SUE   No. Anyway, that isn't what I wanted to talk about. It's our visitor.

STEPHEN   ...?

SUE   In the church.

STEPHEN   Right...

SUE   I see he's still in residence.

STEPHEN   Is it really such a problem?

SUE   Well, that's for you to decide but people aren't happy.

STEPHEN   People?

SUE   Parishioners, people in the village.

STEPHEN   I'm just trying to offer some hospitality.

SUE   By turning the church into something it's not.

STEPHEN   Is it for the village to say what the church should be?

SUE   Is it for you?

STEPHEN   It's for me to try and follow Christ's teaching and hope others might do likewise.

SUE   The church is not a doss house, Stephen.

STEPHEN   And nor is it a private chapel. We're charged by the Gospels –

SUE   You'll just encourage people.

STEPHEN Let's hope you're right. Encourage them to know the love of God.

SUE Cupboard love. Is that the same thing?

STEPHEN In my father's house there are many mansions.

SUE That's as maybe, but in this village, just the one church. People want it to be a place where they can come to commune with God, not rub shoulders with – well, that's just it, you don't know who you'll find.

STEPHEN You talk as if we'd been invaded. It's one man – one man down on his luck, I grant you, but just one man.

SUE For the moment, but if more come – and I know you won't approve of my saying this, but I will say it because it's true and what a lot of people are thinking – if more come, and they will if they think they'll find an open door, it'll affect property prices. *(Beat)* Yes, I knew you'd wrinkle your nose, Stephen, but people have worked hard to make this village what it is. A decent place for decent people.

STEPHEN Surely, all God's children have a right to be welcomed into His house.

SUE Rights are something you earn, Stephen.

STEPHEN Yes.

SUE So when all God's children make a contribution to the greater good – and I'm not talking about money necessarily – then perhaps I'll agree with you.

STEPHEN Christ died for us all, Sue, regardless of social status or acceptability.

SUE When I want you to remind me of the basis of my faith –

STEPHEN I just mean that when Christ asks us to love our neighbour, I think he means everyone.

SUE Then, you'll have to forgive me for failing miserably.

STEPHEN   We all fail miserably all the time, but that's not to say we shouldn't try.

SUE   And if you're putting the village at risk?

STEPHEN   Some people would say that following Christ is a risky business.

SUE   Would they?

STEPHEN   That in its way his teaching was revolutionary.

SUE   Yes, well, I'm not sure we're quite ready for revolution here in Cobham.

STEPHEN   I'm just trying to do... something. To do what Christ would've done. Is that so wrong?

SUE   No, it isn't wrong. But it's a question of context. Nothing exists in a vacuum. It's all very well 'doing good' but there's a price to pay.

STEPHEN   And I'm prepared to pay it.

SUE   But you're asking others to pay it too.

STEPHEN   That's what it means to follow Christ.

SUE   Stephen, I do wish you'd stop telling me what it means to follow Christ.

STEPHEN   I appreciate your long association with the church and believe me I'm hugely grateful for all the work you do and have done over the years but sometimes things have to change.

SUE   Why?

STEPHEN   Because the world changes and the Church is part of the world.

SUE   So it's all right, is it, to have vagrants sleeping in the pews and urinating in the graveyard? *(Beat)* Yes.

STEPHEN   Are you sure about that?

SUE   When Mrs Cook was putting the dead flowers on the compost heap she said she could smell it.

STEPHEN Right.

SUE *(beat)* I don't know what you expect of me, Stephen. I support the church – financially, give my time as a warden, attend regularly – and I have to say I rather object to being told that I'm not up to scratch. If that's the case – and, as you say, we're all miserable failures – I would have thought it was something between me and my God.

STEPHEN I just meant if you could... that it can actually be rewarding if we can find it in our hearts to be a little more... giving.

SUE I'd say I've given my fair share one way and another, wouldn't you? I gave my son. Or don't you think that's quite enough?

STEPHEN God gave His son, too.

SUE Well, I'd say that makes us just about quits.

Sue goes.

STEPHEN Oh, bugger, bugger, bugger, bugger, bugger!

We hear the door slam. Mel appears.

STEPHEN Don't say anything.

Eleven: The Churchyard

Mr Soward with his flask by Ellen's grave.

JACK Well, he's still under the weather. He's not not eating but he's not eating so much and he won't touch those biscuits – you know the ones he likes – so I'm wondering if it might be his teeth. Have to get him some dentures! We can go halves on the Steradent!

And he's sleeping a lot. But then I've to remember he's getting older like the rest of us. *(Beat)* I'll keep him in for a while longer, see how he goes. If he's no better in a week or so I'll get the vet. See what he thinks.

And there's a young fella, have you seen him? Ex army, I think he said. On the road, now. Reckons you gave him some Shepherd's Pie one time. Vicar's been letting him sleep in the church. We had a cup of tea. I wonder if you miss tea? Or do you have it up there?

And did you see the vicar the other day, admiring your new friend? I can never decide what I think of him. He looks worn out half the time. Mind, he was saying he's in charge over Downham now and they've trouble with the gutters. That'll cost.

Well, that's me done. Sausage and mash for tea. Not like yours but it's done in five minutes and you can eat it out of the tray thing so you've no washing up. Just your knife and fork like. Might see if I can tempt Buster with a bit of the sausage. *(Beat)* And now I've to go again! Honestly! I'd go to the doctor but I'd rather not know, you know... I'll just nip round by the compost heap. There's no one to notice.

He kisses his hand and touches the grave.

Twelve: The Vicarage

The sound of a tumble dryer. Mel enters.

MEL Stephen?

She puts down her bag and turns to see Kevin enter in a towel and drying his hair.

MEL Oh!

KEVIN Sorry. Sorry.

MEL Who the hell are −?

KEVIN Sorry. Kevin.

MEL   Kevin?

KEVIN   I've been sleeping in... The vicar's been letting me – Are you his wife?

MEL   What?

KEVIN   His wife. Are you...?

MEL   Yes. Yes, I am. So where's Stephen?

KEVIN   I think he's just drying my clothes. I was having a bath...

MEL   Right...

KEVIN   And he was good enough to...

They look at one another in silence then Stephen enters with Kevin's clothes and some of his own... including a waterproof jacket and a new pair of hiking boots.

STEPHEN   Oh, Mel! You're back.

MEL   Yes.

STEPHEN   Early.

MEL   Yes.

STEPHEN   This is –

MEL   Kevin. Yes. We've met.

STEPHEN   He was just –

MEL   Having a bath. I can see.

STEPHEN   Yes. *(To Kevin)* Anyhow, your things are dry so you can...

KEVIN   Right.

STEPHEN   Use my study, if you like. On the right by the door.

KEVIN   Right. Thanks.

STEPHEN   I looked out a couple of things...

KEVIN   There was no need.

STEPHEN   Just stuff I don't wear, you know.

KEVIN   Right. Thanks. I'll go and get –

STEPHEN   It's just on the right.

Kevin goes. Pause.

MEL   Was that your new waterproof? And the matching boots I bought for us both?

STEPHEN   When do I get time for walking these days? You've still got yours... I didn't think you'd mind.

MEL   Really? Well I do. And I'll tell you what else I mind: I mind coming home to find strangers – strange men – half naked strange men – swanning about my kitchen.

STEPHEN   He was just having a bath.

MEL   Yes, and you were just washing his clothes.

STEPHEN   Is that bad?

MEL   In our washing machine.

STEPHEN   Look, he's leaving today so I asked if he'd like a bath. I didn't think you'd be back so I thought it would be OK.

MEL   And?

STEPHEN   And as he was having a bath, I said I'd put his stuff through a quick wash and – This isn't like you.

MEL   What isn't?

STEPHEN   I mean I can see it was a bit of a shock, him walking in on you but all this about him having a bath and my putting *his* clothes in *our* washing machine... this isn't like you. What is it? What's the matter?

Pause.

MEL   I keep thinking about Wednesday.

STEPHEN   Ah...

MEL   I've not even started the drugs yet and I'm already stressed out. I mean why should it work this time if it's not worked before?

STEPHEN   Hey, come on! *Nil desperandum.* Doctor what's-his-face – the last one ...

MEL   Carter –

STEPHEN   Said it might still happen naturally.

MEL   Yeah, as he waved us good bye.

STEPHEN   Well...

MEL   I think his exact words were: 'You never know: miracles can happen!'

STEPHEN   And, he's right.

MEL   Yes, well you would say that.

STEPHEN   Come here.

She goes to him.

MEL   I'm not even sure I can face it. Starting the whole thing all over, seeing a new doctor, all the tests, the tablets, hoping, waiting and then what if it doesn't happen?

STEPHEN *(beat)* Actually, about Wednesday...

She pulls away.

MEL   What?

STEPHEN   I'm really sorry...

MEL   What?

STEPHEN   I've got a funeral.

MEL   What!

STEPHEN   Sorry.

MEL   Whose?

STEPHEN   Mrs Melrose.

MEL   Who?

STEPHEN   Over in Barton.

MEL   Stephen!

STEPHEN   I know.

MEL   It's your day off!

STEPHEN   It's the only day her son could make it.

MEL   Oh, well, I'd hate to inconvenience anyone.

STEPHEN   He's coming from Scotland.

MEL   Good for him.

STEPHEN   What do you want me to do?

MEL   I want you to put me and our chances of having a baby ahead of your bloody job for once.

STEPHEN   Well, it's not just a job, is it?

MEL   Don't give me that... that's your get-out-of-gaol-free-card. No. I'm sorry. No. I'm not having it.

Kevin enters, dressed and wearing Stephen's new boots and jacket.

KEVIN   What do you reckon? *(Beat)* Oh. Sorry.

STEPHEN   No.

KEVIN   I'm just about ready for the off.

STEPHEN   Right. Would you like me to give you a lift anywhere?

MEL   Pah!

KEVIN   No. No, I'll be fine. Looking forward to being back on the road.

STEPHEN   Where are you heading?

KEVIN   Dunno. North...

STEPHEN   Well, I hope it all goes well for you. And if in doubt...

KEVIN   Sing!

STEPHEN   That's right.

KEVIN *(referring to the boots)* You sure about these?

STEPHEN   Course. Yeah.

KEVIN   Right then, I'll be saying goodbye. Sorry about earlier, you know –

MEL   It's fine.

KEVIN   Right then. Thanks for everything and, you know, the...

STEPHEN   No worries. You take care of yourself. *(Beat)* And God bless you.

KEVIN   You too.

Kevin goes.

MEL   Did you give him money? *(Beat)* You did, didn't you?

STEPHEN   He didn't have any.

MEL   How much?

STEPHEN   Not much.

MEL   Well, I hope not Stephen, cos we're supposed to be saving up, remember?

STEPHEN   Of course I remember.

MEL   You'll be telling me next that the poor are always with us.

STEPHEN   Well, they are.

MEL   Thank you Saint Francis of Assisi.

STEPHEN   Let's not have a row, eh?

MEL   It's a bit late for that.

STEPHEN   All right, then, let's have one.

MEL   All right. You want to help the poor and homeless, you give what you can to established charities who know what they're doing. You know it's the best way to do it – you know that – Christ! It used to be your job telling people just that –

STEPHEN   Mel, please –

MEL   You do not – repeat, *not* – bring people into my house, give them free rein and then send them on their way with our money in their pockets and a brand new jacket and boots.

STEPHEN   The Gospels tell us to welcome strangers, feed the hungry, clothe the naked.

MEL   Yes, and stone adulterers.

STEPHEN   That's the Old –

MEL   We have standing orders, Stephen, eight, nine standing orders to charities whose work we both support. You can't just go round helping everyone, willy nilly.

STEPHEN   So you pass the buck?

MEL   No. You do what you can, when you can.

STEPHEN   And that's all I'm talking about. Here was a chap – a young chap – needed a bit of help. And so I helped him. And you know what? It felt good. Like I was actually making a difference.

MEL   You see, it's all about you feeling good!

STEPHEN   No!

MEL   Well, that's what it sounds like.

STEPHEN *(beat)* I don't know what you want me to say.

MEL   How about sorry?

STEPHEN   What am I supposed to have done?

MEL   You don't get it, do you?

STEPHEN   If it's about Wednesday –

MEL   Pah!

STEPHEN   I can only spread my self so thin.

MEL   Cue the violins.

STEPHEN   What's that supposed to mean?

MEL   It means I've had enough of hearing how hard things are for you. Because you know what? I know they are Stephen, I know. But this was your choice, not mine, yours and I've done my best to go along with it and help you make it happen because, as you never tire of reminding me, it's your *calling*. But I am sick to the back teeth of your calling having to be my calling and the phone going all hours and people coming round and everybody having an opinion about everything we do.

Pause.

STEPHEN   I've got a sermon to prepare.

He goes.

MEL   Well, God bless you.

She picks up Kevin's disgarded towel...

The man walking...

End of Part One.

PART TWO: EASTER

Thirteen: Palm Sunday

In the vicarage, Mel is going through bank statements. In the church, Stephen is washing Kevin's feet.

KEVIN   Verily I say unto you, inasmuch as you have done it unto one of the least of these my brethren, ye have done it unto me.

Stephen looks at him .

KEVIN   Matthew Twenty-five.

STEPHEN *(beat)* I'll be doing plenty of it on Thursday.

KEVIN   You don't mind? Other people's feet.

STEPHEN   It's no more than Christ did for the apostles.

Stephen dries Kevin's feet.

MEL   Never really wanted kids when I was young. Never really thought about it and then... I don't know... Meeting Stephen, getting older... God knows, it wasn't for want of trying but it just didn't happen. And the more it didn't happen, the more I wanted – needed – had to have a baby. So we had all the tests – oh joy! – and there was no reason I shouldn't be getting pregnant – no reason they could find ... I just wasn't. We thought about adopting but for me it wasn't so much about having a *baby* as *having* a baby. So we started with IVF and managed to get two cycles on the NHS but... No...

STEPHEN   There.

KEVIN   Thank you.

Kevin puts his socks back on. Stephen looks at Kevin's boots.

STEPHEN   How've they been?

KEVIN   Yeah, great.

STEPHEN   They'll've done a bit of walking since I saw you last.

KEVIN   Just a bit!

STEPHEN   Well, I'm glad they brought you back to St. Peter's.

KEVIN   Yeah.

STEPHEN   You're welcome to stay, of course but it's a busy week – Holy Week – you might have to look out for yourself.

KEVIN   Not a problem. Would you like me to do yours?

STEPHEN   No! No, don't worry about that.

KEVIN   I'd like to.

STEPHEN   Really...?

KEVIN   Return the favour.

STEPHEN   OK. All right. Why not?

Kevin washes Stephen's feet.

MEL   So we saved up to go private. Why I thought it should work just cos we were paying for it I've no idea. Maybe the hormones... You do go a bit mad, become addicted to on-line fertility forums. But I was so sure. So sure. Even bought some baby clothes. Stupid, I know... Anyway it definitely won't be more than five grand this time. Probably. They tell you not to worry, that stress can be your worst enemy. And you smile and nod and want to scream. I'm not sure Stephen feels the same but then I don't feel about God the way he does. Well, you can't just feel something if you don't feel it, can you?

Mel spots an anomaly in the statement.

Kevin dries Stephen's feet.

STEPHEN   Thank you.

KEVIN   Like you say, what Christ did.

STEPHEN   Yes.

Pause. Stephen puts his socks back on.

STEPHEN   It's a bit colder than when you were last here.

KEVIN   End of November.

STEPHEN   Advent.

KEVIN   And your wife, is she...?

STEPHEN   Yes, she's well. Well, yes she's... yes.

KEVIN   No news on the baby front? *(Beat)* You mentioned you'd been trying.

STEPHEN   Did I? Oh... No. Still no luck, I'm afraid.

KEVIN   I hope I didn't cause a row, you know last time...

STEPHEN   No, no, we were... No...

KEVIN   Good. *(Pause)* And there was an old chap. *(Beat)* Came to see to his wife's grave every day.

STEPHEN   Oh, Mr Soward! *(Beat)* Actually, no, he's not been very well, I don't think. Well, he's not been for a few days and I've been meaning to pop round. I'm glad you reminded me.

KEVIN   Say hello from me if you see him.

STEPHEN   Yes. Yes, I'll do that. *(Beat)* He was telling me you were in the army.

KEVIN   Was he?

STEPHEN   Where were you?

KEVIN   In the thick of it...

STEPHEN   Lose any friends?

KEVIN   It happens.

STEPHEN   That must be terriblc.

KEVIN   It is.

STEPHEN *(beat)* Did you ever... you know, did you ever have to...

KEVIN   Do what soldiers do? It's what they're trained for. Stuff needs doing, they do it. Oh, not for Queen and country. Not for freedom or democracy or any of that crap. For their mates: the ones who've been killed, the ones who've been blown apart and survived, the ones who carry it about in their heads... They do it for them.

STEPHEN   You'd wonder why we've still not learned it doesn't work.

KEVIN   Don't get me started on the fucking politicians.

STEPHEN   No.

KEVIN   Sorry.

STEPHEN *(beat)* Right. I've left you a blanket. And there's a heater in the vestry, if you need it. You might be better sleeping in there, actually – warmer.

KEVIN   I'll be fine. Better than them poor buggers in... Where is it?

STEPHEN *(beat)* Oh, the earthquake, yes. Terrible that. All those people... children...

KEVIN   Makes you think.

STEPHEN   Yes.

KEVIN   Makes you grateful for what you've got. *(Beat)* Well, thanks for the pedicure.

STEPHEN   And mine.

Stephen goes. Kevin wraps the blanket about him.

He breathes in slowly. And out...

Fourteen: Sue & Jack

Sue gives Jack something wrapped in a blanket.

SUE   I'm very sorry, Mr Soward.

JACK	Where did you find him?
SUE	In the church yard.
JACK	I had the door open, burned some toast... He must've... Been calling him up and down the lane.
SUE	He was... by your wife's grave.
JACK	Was he really?
SUE	As if he'd just gone to sleep.
JACK	I'n't that something?
SUE	Must've been a good age.
JACK	Sixteen nearly. And he'd not been well, you know.
SUE	Still, it's never easy.
JACK	It's the company.
SUE	Yes. I don't know where I'd be with out my two.
JACK	You've Labradors, haven't you?
SUE	Mother and son.
JACK	Keep you fit, I expect – all that walking.
SUE	I like to keep active. *(Beat)* Perhaps you should...
JACK	Yes. Yes, I'll just...

Jack lays down his burden.

JACK	Is this your blanket?
SUE	Not to worry... Just one I keep in the car.
JACK	I'll get it back to you.
SUE	Really...

Pause.

JACK	Your Alex was always fond of him.
SUE	Yes.

JACK   And we were very fond of *him*. *(Beat)* He loved my Ellen's fruit loaf.

SUE   I was never much of a one for baking.

JACK   Butter that thick!

SUE   I know he liked coming here.

JACK   We never had any of our own.

Pause.

JACK   How's your husband? I've not seen –

SUE   No. He doesn't get out much now.

JACK   I miss Ellen, you know, but you expect it, don't you, when folk are getting on? But your lad...

SUE   Yes.

JACK   Seems wrong.

SUE   I should really be getting back...

JACK   Aye.

SUE   Will you be all right, you know with..?

JACK   Oh... Aye... Aye.

SUE   There was a card in the village shop... New Lane, I think it was – a litter of collies.

JACK   I don't think I'll be getting another. Not now.

SUE   No.

JACK   You can't just replace them, can you?

SUE   No. No, you can't.

Fifteen: The Vicarage

MEL   He's back then?

STEPHEN   Is that a problem?

MEL   Not unless you're planning to give him the run of the house and another fifty quid.

STEPHEN *(beat)* I told him he could use the sink in the vestry if he wanted a wash.

MEL   I wouldn't mention that to Sue.

STEPHEN   None of her business.

MEL   Not sure I'd open with that line of defence.

STEPHEN   I don't see why I should have to defend myself in the first place.

MEL   I expect she worries about security. Isn't that what church wardens do?

STEPHEN   That's not the reason! Anyway, what's with you, siding with the enemy?

MEL   Not siding with anyone. Just saying.

Pause.

STEPHEN   All right, what have I done?

Mel produces the bank statement.

STEPHEN *(beat)* Oh.

MEL   Yeah. Standing orders to two more charities and an increase in the rest...

STEPHEN   I thought you approved of –

MEL   We're supposed to be saving up.

STEPHEN   That doesn't mean other people don't need our help all of a sudden.

MEL   Oh, right. And you didn't mention this because...?

STEPHEN   Because... *(Beat)* I knew you'd make a fuss.

MEL   Fuss?

STEPHEN   Which you are.

MEL   I have been working... *(Beat)* It's bad enough getting ready for the next round of hormones and worrying about all of that without...

STEPHEN   Well, we don't have to.

MEL   What?

STEPHEN   I mean, no-one's forcing us, are they?

MEL   Sometimes Stephen... I just don't... I think I do but then I don't.

STEPHEN   What?

MEL   Understand what goes on in your head.

STEPHEN   I just mean... Well, it wouldn't be the end of the world, would it?

MEL   No?

STEPHEN   I mean when you think of... You know, people caught up in that earthquake – the children...

MEL *(beat)*   Where's this come from?

STEPHEN   Nowhere. It's on the news... Something Kevin said.

MEL   Oh well then!

STEPHEN   Don't be like that.

MEL   Not being like anything. It's just... If you could hear yourself sometimes!

STEPHEN   What?

MEL   I mean considering you really don't know him from Adam, and you've not seen him for months, you do talk about him quite a bit.

STEPHEN   Do I?

MEL   Yes.

STEPHEN   Well, he made quite an impact on me last time he was here.

MEL   Obviously.

STEPHEN   What does that mean?

MEL   I don't *know*. You'd think you were in love with him or something.

STEPHEN   Don't be ridiculous.

MEL   Well, *I* don't know!

STEPHEN   Mel!

MEL   There was that boy at school!

STEPHEN   What?

MEL   When you were at school.

STEPHEN   Who? *(Beat)* I was fourteen!

MEL   You were in love with *him*.

STEPHEN   Yeah, like I say, I was fourteen. I was in love with anyone who didn't beat me up. He didn't even know about it. Or he would've beaten me up, I expect.

MEL   You're not fourteen now.

STEPHEN   No, I'm not. And I'm not in love with Kevin.

MEL   You don't find him attractive?

STEPHEN   Why do you?

MEL   Don't be – *(Beat)* Now who's being ridiculous?

STEPHEN   You tell me. *(Pause)* Just... I find him very... interesting. When I'm with him... Things he does... Says... Just makes me think...

MEL   What?

STEPHEN *(beat)* Of Jesus.

MEL   Christ! It's worst than I thought. Tell me you don't think – Please tell me you don't think he's Jesus.

STEPHEN   Course I don't! I'm not saying that.

MEL   Then what are you saying?

STEPHEN   That he makes me remember what following Christ is all about. Why I wanted to do it. Who I am. What I'm for. *(Beat)* That I'm not a total waste of space.

MEL   I thought what you were for was me… Us.

STEPHEN   Course it is.

MEL   Doesn't feel like that sometimes.

STEPHEN   Just… Helping others… know you're helping others.

MEL   What is it they say about Charity?

STEPHEN   OK.

MEL   We've got plans, remember?

STEPHEN   Course.

MEL   So priorities, Stephen**…** Yeah?

STEPHEN   Yeah… Friends…?

She's about to take his proffered hands when the phone rings.

Pause.

STEPHEN   It might be important. *(He answers the phone)* / Hello? Yes. Yes, it is… Oh, I'm sorry to hear that, Mr Soward… Yes, of course I can… Yes, of course.

MEL   / Fine. Answer it then. *(Going)* As long as we're clear…

STEPHEN   Mel! Bugger. No, Mr Soward, not… Yes. Yes, I'll pop round. Tomorrow? Yes. Yes, and I'm very sorry.

Sixteen: Monday of Holy Week
Kevin washes, stripped to the waist and singing to himself.

KEVIN   My song is love unknown, My Saviour's love to me;

Love to the loveless shown, That they might lovely be.
O who am I, that for my sake My Lord should take, frail flesh and die?

Sue puts flowers on her son's grave.

Jack packs away Buster's things.

Mel watches Kevin as he washes.

He turns but she's gone.

Seventeen: Jack's house

Stephen and Jack.

JACK   Do you remember when my Ellen died?

STEPHEN   Just after I arrived, wasn't it?

JACK   You came to see me.

STEPHEN   Yes.

JACK   Only been here five minutes –

STEPHEN   Well –

JACK   But you came and sat with me.

STEPHEN   It was the least I could do.

JACK   Sat with me and watched *Countdown*.

STEPHEN   Greater love hath no man!

JACK   It was what I needed. I didn't want you laying down your life! Where would that have got us? *(Beat)* Mind, you're right, *Countdown's* not what it was. Not since whatsisname died and Carol Vordeman left.

STEPHEN   I've never really followed it.

JACK   Don't suppose you've a lot of time for telly.

STEPHEN   I like to watch the football sometimes.

JACK   Aye. Ellen couldn't be doing with it. She liked the show jumping – you know the horses... Harvey Smith! He was a bad lad, wa'n't he?

STEPHEN   Was he?

JACK   Oh, yes but she liked him cos he wa'n't as la-di-dah as the rest. Still, there was no need to do what he did.

STEPHEN   No?

JACK   I don't think so. If we all went round letting off steam, where would it end?

STEPHEN   I'm not sure it doesn't help sometimes to get things off your chest.

JACK   But there are ways and ways, aren't there?

STEPHEN   I expect you're right.

JACK   And do you know what else she couldn't be doing with?

STEPHEN   What's that?

JACK   *Can't Cook, Won't Cook.* She used to say, Well, don't cook then! *(They laugh. Pause.)* Terrible what's happening with that earthquake.

STEPHEN   Yes.

JACK   You wonder what He's thinking sometimes, don't you?

STEPHEN   You do.

JACK   Vicar –

STEPHEN   Stephen –

JACK   Aye. Can I ask you something?

STEPHEN   Fire away.

JACK *(pulling out a revolver)* I'm in two minds, you see.

STEPHEN *(beat)* Is that loaded?

JACK　　　Aye. But not primed, don't worry.

STEPHEN *(transfixed)* Right...

JACK　　　Course when Ellen went... It was a mercy in a way but... Well, there was Buster, wa'n't there? I couldn't just give up. He needed walking, feeding... But now...

STEPHEN　　Yes.

JACK　　　I don't know what to do. I mean, I know what I'd like to do but I keep thinking, what would Ellen say? With her being a church-goer. And I wouldn't want to cause any bother, and it would be a bother, wouldn't it, when you think about it – the practicalities and that... so what do you reckon?

STEPHEN *(beat)* I reckon we should... see how things go. See how you feel in a week or two... Think things over... Maybe see the doctor?

JACK　　　I'm not one for doctors.

STEPHEN　　No. *(Beat)* We could pray if you like.

JACK　　　I'll leave that to you.

STEPHEN　　Yes. And in the meantime... Why don't you let me look after that?

JACK *(beat)*　Have you handled a gun before?

STEPHEN *(beat)* No.

JACK　　　Well, I don't know. I wouldn't want to put you out.

STEPHEN　　You wouldn't be, really. And I think it might be for the best, just until...

JACK　　　I decide what to do.

STEPHEN　　Yes. Maybe if you just, you know...

JACK　　　Oh, aye... *(Removes the magazine)* Shall I give you the cartridges too?

STEPHEN   No, you keep them. Maybe safer that way...

JACK   If you think so.

STEPHEN   I do. Yes. I *(Pause)* Is there anywhere you could go? Anyone you could visit, even for a day or two?

JACK *(beat)* I've a sister near Grantham. We don't... She never really got on with Ellen. You lose touch.

STEPHEN   You know, if I were you, I'd give her a ring, see how she's fixed. I bet she'd love to see you.

JACK   Well...

STEPHEN   It's worth thinking about.

JACK   Aye.

Pause.

STEPHEN   Well –

JACK   Before you go, Vicar –

STEPHEN   Stephen.

JACK   Aye... *(Fetching something wrapped in a blanket)* I was wondering... Would you bury him? I'm not sure I could...

STEPHEN *(taking the body of the dog)* No, of course.

JACK   Somewhere, you know...

STEPHEN   Yes.

JACK   And maybe say a prayer...

Stephen nods.

Eighteen: Sue

Sue walking her dogs again, throwing balls for them to fetch.

SUE   Easter. Not that it feels much like Spring...

Go on! Snow in some parts apparently. And even here... Bitter. I can't help thinking on nights like that... how cold the earth must be...

Good boy! Good boy!

I know he's dead. I know that. Knew the moment I answered the door and saw the officer... But I still hear him sometimes... playing the piano – I kept all his music – or the funny chattering noise he'd make after a bath when he was little... jumping and jiggling all over the place as I dried his hair...

Or I go into his room – we've kept it just as it was, you know – and... Well, he was never very tidy – even after Sandhurst – his father could never understand it – and I throw things about, open the drawers and... socks, shirts... Then later, I go back, clear up the mess as if...

Or I sit. Sit and wait for him to come tearing up the stairs and pop his head round the door with that look of his... He doesn't, of course. Of course he doesn't. But I go on waiting.

Come on, Dixie... Good boy...

Nineteen: Good Friday

In the vicarage, Mel pours herself a drink. Stephen enters.

STEPHEN	You're drinking.
MEL	So I am.
STEPHEN	But –
MEL	Yes?
STEPHEN	I don't...
MEL	My card was declined. Tell me you didn't...

Pause.

STEPHEN   You saw the pictures in the paper.

MEL   Yes and they were terrible, shocking –

STEPHEN   Sickening –

MEL   Yes!

STEPHEN   So what are we supposed to do? Nothing?

MEL *(beat)*   I don't know what to say to you. I don't know what to say. It's like you've gone mad.

STEPHEN   Is it mad to want to help children lying in their own excrement, covered in flies?

MEL   No.

STEPHEN   Well then?

MEL   That was our money – ours – mine actually but anyway not yours – not yours to do with as you see fit.

STEPHEN   But do we really need it?

MEL   What?

STEPHEN   I mean we don't really *need* it, do we?

MEL   Don't we? I do. I need it. I need it to have a baby.

STEPHEN   I know, yeah, of course, yeah but is that a need?

MEL   I'm sorry?

STEPHEN   I mean is that a *need* or a *want*?

MEL   Well, I don't know. I thought it was both. I thought we *needed* it because we *wanted* to have a baby. But maybe I'm wrong.

STEPHEN   No!

MEL   Then what the hell were you thinking?

STEPHEN   I was trying to think what Christ would do.

MEL   Oh, and would Christ give away our IVF money?

STEPHEN   If someone needed it more, yes.

MEL   Then he'd be an insensitive thieving bastard too. *(Beat)* Stephen, you can't take the needs of the whole world on your shoulders.

STEPHEN   Jesus did.

MEL   I'm sick of bloody Jesus.

STEPHEN   Please don't say that.

MEL   Well I am. And you're not Jesus, are you?

STEPHEN   No.

MEL   No, you're not. So give it a rest.

STEPHEN   I'm not sure I can.

MEL   And I'm not sure how much more I can take. This is my life, our life, not the gospels, not a Bible story – our life, our future. *(Beat)* Four grand, Stephen. Four bloody grand!

STEPHEN   We can save up again.

MEL   Oh, can *we*?

STEPHEN   All right, I know it's you –

MEL   That's right, it is. *(Pause)* But that's not the point, is it?

STEPHEN   I don't know.

MEL   This isn't about money.

STEPHEN   What is it then?

MEL   I think it's about whether you want this baby at all.

STEPHEN *(beat)* Course I do.

MEL   Maybe that's been the problem all along.

STEPHEN   What are you saying? That it's my fault? That it's mind over matter or something stupid? And just because... Bloody hell, I wish that's how things worked... my life would be a damn sight easier.

MEL   You've hardly been near me.

STEPHEN   We had sex the other week!

MEL   I practically had to force you.

STEPHEN   You know what it's like in the run up to Easter.

MEL   You'll be telling me next you've got a headache.

STEPHEN   Yes, well, having to perform on cue because you're ovulating isn't exactly the world's greatest aphrodisiac.

MEL   You don't have to wait till I'm ovulating.

STEPHEN   Is that what this is all about? Not getting enough? All right, come on! Come on then ! If that's what you want, I'll give it you, you can have it.

He forces her to kiss him. She resists. Sue enters.

SUE   Oh, I'm sorry, I did knock.

MEL   Not to worry. I'd say we were just about finished, wouldn't you?

She goes. Pause.

SUE   Perhaps I should...

STEPHEN   No. No... how can I help you?

SUE   Well, I don't like to say I told you so, Stephen...

STEPHEN   Sorry?

SUE   Our visitor is back I see.

STEPHEN   He's passing by, that's all.

SUE   And he just happened to drop in, did he?

STEPHEN   He came –

SUE   Because he knew he wouldn't be turned away. This is what happens when you encourage people: they take advantage.

STEPHEN   I dare say he'll only be with us a day or two.

SUE   Until the next time. And who knows how many more there might be then.

STEPHEN   He just wants somewhere to rest on his journey.

SUE   Well, I hope you're right, but if it's all the same to you, I'd like to empty the disaster fund appeal box. Just to be on the safe side.

STEPHEN   Do you really think –? *(Beat)* I'll get the key. It's in my study.

Twenty: The Church

Kevin sits in silence. Mel enters, still drinking. She watches him. After a time Kevin turns.

KEVIN   Oh!

MEL   Your turn to be surprised.

KEVIN   Yes. We can't go on meeting like this.

MEL   At least you've got your pants on this time.

KEVIN   Yes. *(Pause)* After a bit of peace and quiet?

MEL   Something like that.

KEVIN   Well, you've come to the right place.

Pause.

MEL   My husband thinks you're Jesus.

KEVIN   Does he?

MEL   More or less.

KEVIN   And what do you think?

MEL   Oh, I leave all that sort of thing to him.

KEVIN *(beat)* Where is he?

MEL   If you mean does he know I'm here – no, he doesn't. Deep in conversation with the Lovely Sue. Important church business I expect. *(Proffering the bottle)* Can I tempt you?

KEVIN   I don't.

MEL   Neither do I. Trying to have a baby.

KEVIN   Your husband said.

MEL   Did he?

KEVIN   Yes.

MEL   And did he say we're not having much luck?

KEVIN   That must be hard. You could do with one of those angelic visitations. You know... And lo! She was with child...

She looks at him. Perhaps he's framed against the window, as Stephen first saw him. She goes to him.

MEL   Hold me. Please.

He opens his arms. They embrace. She lifts her face. They kiss briefly. Then Mel kisses Kevin passionately, hungrily, thankfully... Stephen and Sue enter and see them. Eventually, Mel realises they are there and breaks away. She looks at Stephen. He gives the key to Sue and goes into the vestry. Pause. Mel goes. Sue and Kevin face one another.

SUE   People like you make me sick. You're like a plague in the lives of decent people, taking advantage of their better nature, abusing their hospitality. You defile a holy place, while other people... decent people... young men...

She goes to the collection box and tries to unlock it. Eventually she loses patience and breaks open the lid. About to go, she stops and addresses Kevin.

SUE   My son... My son died... gave his life while you roam the country living off hand-outs, taking what you can and giving nothing back. Twenty-four years old... Doing his duty... And people like you are still alive.

KEVIN   He was a soldier.

SUE   He was an officer.

KEVIN   Captain Alexander Hunt.

SUE   How do you -? How dare you even... ? You're not fit to speak his name.

KEVIN   I was there.

SUE   Where?

KEVIN   At the end... I was with him.

SUE   Don't give me that!

KEVIN   He was thinking of you, speaking of you, how much he missed you, loved you.

A silence.

SUE   It was our fault.

KEVIN   No, you mustn't think –

SUE   We made –

KEVIN   He wanted to be there. He loved his job, his men.

Sue weeps.

SUE   You were with him?

KEVIN   Always.

SUE   Did he –?

KEVIN   No. No, when it came it was quick.

SUE   And he didn't...

KEVIN   Never. No. He loved you.

Pause.

SUE   Losing him was... Giving birth was nothing by comparison. *(Beat)* He always loved music... but the army was a family tradition so in the end he followed my husband into the regiment.

The day they brought us the news... I'd never seen my

husband cry before. Perhaps it's worse for men – for soldiers. And all I could think was how he'd be missing Christmas and how cross that would make him because he loved all the preparations and... Imagine that. Imagine thinking that. It's been two years. I've tried to find comfort in prayer, in the Gospels... Perhaps now we can have some peace. *(Beat)* I have to... my husband... Would you take this – look after it till Stephen... Thank you. Thank you.

She goes, leaving Kevin with the broken collection box. Stephen enters from the vestry.

STEPHEN   What are you doing?

Kevin is silent.

STEPHEN   What are you doing with that?

Kevin is silent.

STEPHEN   Give it to me.

Kevin hands over the box.

STEPHEN   Is this how you repay me? Is this the thanks I get for taking you in? Well? Is it? People have given that money out of the goodness of their heart. Decent people trying to help those less fortunate than themselves. And you come along and just... Well? Have you nothing to say?

Kevin is silent.

STEPHEN   I'm going to have to ask you to leave.

Kevin picks up his bag.

STEPHEN   You betrayed my trust. I'm sorry.

Kevin starts to go...

STEPHEN   Well, say something!

KEVIN   God bless.

Twenty-one: Decisions

Sue packing away Alex's music.

Mel packing a case. Jack with his suitcase.

JACK   I hadn't seen her since the funeral. Didn't speak much even then. What was there to say? They'd never got on and as far as she was concerned I'd taken Ellen's side which I had, of course.

But I'm glad the vicar put the idea in my head cos I'd never've done it otherwise and it was good to see her again. She doesn't half look like my mother now. We didn't talk much. But she has a Yorkie so we took him out. To the park, you know.

And she said she'll try and get down in the summer. So that's something to look forward to. Still, I'll be glad to be home. Might do a bit of tidying up in the shed.

He goes.

Sue finishes her task.

Mel takes out a pregnancy testing kit.

Twenty-two: Easter Sunday

Stephen rushes in looking for his keys.

STEPHEN   Where the hell did I put them..?

Mel enters.

MEL   Stephen!

STEPHEN   I'm not being funny, Mel, but Sue's on her way and I can't find my bloody keys.

MEL   We need to talk.

STEPHEN   Can it wait? I should be back by... oh, two at the latest, we'll talk then, yeah?

MEL   It won't take –

The phone rings.

STEPHEN   Bloody hell!

MEL   Stephen!

STEPHEN   It's probably Sue wondering where I am. (*Stephen picks up the phone.*)

MEL   I think I'm pregnant.

STEPHEN *(beat)* What?

MEL   I think I'm pregnant.

Stephen replaces the receiver.

STEPHEN   How do you –?

Mel produces a pregnancy testing wand.

STEPHEN   You sure?

MEL   Yes. No. I don't know. I just... I think so, yes.

STEPHEN   My God... This is...

MEL   Like a miracle?

Silence... then Jack bursts in.

JACK   Vicar!

STEPHEN   Mr Soward!

JACK   I'm sorry to burst in like this but it's that feller.

STEPHEN   Who?

JACK   The one was staying in the church.

MEL   Kevin?

JACK   Is that his name?

STEPHEN   What about him?

JACK   I was at my sister's, like you suggested – just since Friday – and I wanted to get back with the weather and that and then just now, when I went out to the shed... There he was.

MEL   Doing what?

JACK   No... No, I think he's dead.

STEPHEN   What?

MEL   Oh my God!

STEPHEN   Have you called the police?

JACK   No.

MEL   And you're sure he's –

JACK   Well, I thought he was asleep but he didn't answer so I shook him. No. He's absolutely cold.

STEPHEN   Right... Mel, I'd better...

MEL   Course.

STEPHEN   Come on, Mr Soward, I'll go back with you.

Sue enters.

SUE   The door was open so I –

STEPHEN   Sorry Sue but I've got to dash. Mel, would you...?

Stephen and Jack go.

SUE   Obviously something important.

MEL   It's Kevin...

SUE   Kevin?

MEL   The bloke who was staying in the church.

SUE   What about him?

MEL   Mr Soward's just found him... dead apparently.

SUE   Oh!

MEL   He must have been sleeping in his shed while he was away.

SUE   I thought... I thought he was sleeping in the church.

MEL   Not since Friday. Stephen caught him taking money. Asked him to leave.

SUE   What money?

MEL   From the appeal box or something.

SUE   Oh!

MEL   What is it?

SUE   This is terrible.

MEL   I know.

SUE   No, I mean... He wasn't taking the money...

MEL   No?

SUE   After you and Stephen left the other day, I had to go so I asked him... This is terrible...

Pause.

MEL   Sue, about the other day –

SUE   It's none of my business.

MEL   No, I know but I'm sorry if it put you in a difficult... Stephen and I have been having a few problems.

SUE   As I say it's none of my business.

Pause.

MEL   I've not exactly been the text book clergy wife, have I?

SUE   Well, it must be difficult with your job and all the commuting.

MEL   Yes.

SUE   And I know how busy Stephen can be. Five parishes! It can't be easy. Father Derek would never have managed.

MEL   I wish you'd tell him that. Sometimes he feels he can't do right for doing wrong.

SUE   I must remember.

Pause.

MEL   We've been trying to start a family. Well, that was the idea.

SUE   Children can be a blessing.

MEL   I'm sorry, I didn't mean... Stephen told me about your son.

SUE   Yes.

MEL   I can't imagine...

SUE   No. *(Beat)* He was such a beautiful baby. And I'd wanted him so badly. My husband can be... difficult... But Alex could be very strong-minded in his way. *(Beat)* Two people who love one another but seem to want different things...

MEL   Yes.

SUE   There were some terrible rows. And you find yourself caught in the middle. I don't mind telling you, I thought of leaving more than once. But you can't just walk out on a marriage, can you? You've made promises. And when you've children... *(Pause)*

Maybe I was wrong. Sometimes it's hard to know what to do for the best. But in the event it's as well I stayed. Since Alex... Well, since he died... I'm not sure my husband would have coped on his own.

MEL   No.

Stephen enters.

MEL   Well?

SUE   Melanie told me, how dreadful.

MEL   Have you called the police?

STEPHEN   No.

SUE   I think perhaps we should.

STEPHEN   He wasn't there.

MEL   What?

SUE   How do you mean?

STEPHEN   We got to the house, went through to the garden, to the shed – and – nothing. No sign.

MEL   But he said –

STEPHEN   I know. Cold.

SUE   Had he just been sleeping then?

STEPHEN   He must've been but Mr Soward was absolutely certain. And he'd locked the shed when he left on Friday.

MEL   So he'd been in there three days?

SUE   You don't think he could've imagined the whole thing?

STEPHEN   I don't know.

MEL   But why would –?

STEPHEN   With his dog dying last week... He was very low. That's why I suggested he went to his sister's.

MEL   And Kevin definitely wasn't there?

STEPHEN   No but you could see he had been. He'd left this...

Stephen has the waterproof jacket he gave Kevin.

SUE   How very odd. Appropriate, I suppose, given the day. *(Pause)* Well, I'll go and open up.

STEPHEN   Yes.

He puts the jacket down. Sue goes. Pause. Mel picks the jacket up.

MEL   How was Mr Soward when you left him?

STEPHEN   A bit embarrassed I think but still convinced of what he'd seen.

MEL   And are you all right?

STEPHEN   Yeah. *(Beat)* I just keep thinking about what you said.

MEL   Yes... *(Pause)* There's something else. *(Beat)* I'm going away.

STEPHEN *(beat)* What d'you mean?

She doesn't reply.

STEPHEN   You're going away, but you're coming back, yeah?

MEL   I don't know.

STEPHEN *(beat)* Is it him?

MEL   Who?

STEPHEN   Kevin. Are you going with him?

MEL   Don't be... Stephen! God, for an intelligent man you can be bloody stupid.

STEPHEN   Can I?

MEL   Yes. No, it's... us... this place... everything. I think it might be best.

STEPHEN   But not now.

MEL   Especially now. *(Beat)* I don't want to be a single parent.

STEPHEN   What?

MEL   I don't want this baby ever to feel you've not got time for it.

STEPHEN   I'd never –

MEL   Like there's something more important you have to do.

STEPHEN   I'd never let that happen. I'd never let my job –

MEL   But it's not just a job, is it?

STEPHEN *(beat)* I never meant –

MEL   No, I know. I know you didn't. But that's how it feels sometimes. How it is.

Sue enters.

SUE   Stephen, people are arriving and I was wondering if I should light the candles.

Pause.

MEL   Yes. Why don't you do that? He'll be right there.

Sue goes.

Mel and Stephen look at one another.

STEPHEN   Wait till I get back yeah? We'll talk.

MEL   I don't know.

STEPHEN   Please.

The organ starts to play...

Twenty-three: Easter Sunday

CHOIR   This joyful Easter-tide, Away with care and sorrow! My Love, the Crucified, Hath sprung to life this morrow.
Had Christ, that once was slain, Ne'er burst His three day prison, Our faith had been in vain;
But now is Christ arisen, Arisen, arisen, arisen!

Stephen faces the congregation.

STEPHEN   And I'm reminded on this Easter Day, when the love of God triumphs over death, of the story Jesus tells in St.

Luke's Gospel and of St Paul's letter to his Hebrew brothers – asking us to place that love at the centre of our lives – to love one another and, in these days of distrust and fear, not to be careful of strangers but rather *care-full*, full of care, welcoming them to our table without thought of return.

Of course the scriptures have been translated and edited many times over the centuries but however we translate and edit them, the idea of love and loving seems to lie at the centre of Christ's teaching. And if we want to spread the Word of God, we do well to remember that the word of God is love: the love of God given by the God of Love.

(He reads)

'Remember those who are in prison, as though in prison with them, and those who are mistreated as though you also feel the blows. Let marriage be held in honour... and the marriage bed undefiled. Keep your life free from love of money, and be content to do good and to share what you have. Let brotherly love continue. Do not neglect to show hospitality to strangers, for thereby some have entertained angels unawares.'

Jack by Ellen's grave.

Mel in the kitchen.

Sue in church

The man walking...

The End.

Aurora Metro Books

some of our other play collections

THREE PLAYS by Jonathan Moore. Introduced by Gregory Hersov
ISBN 0-9536757-2-6 £10.95

GRAEAE PLAYS 1: new plays redefining disability. Selected and
introduced by Jenny Sealey ISBN 0-9536757-6-9 £12.99

BEST OF THE FEST Ed. Phil Setren. Plays from the London New Play
Festival ISBN 0-9515877-8-1 £12.99

NEW SOUTH AFRICAN PLAYS ed. Charles J. Fourie
ISBN 9780954233013 £11.99

BLACK AND ASIAN PLAYS ANTHOLOGY Introduced by Afia Nkrumah
ISBN 0-9536757-4-2 £12.99

BALKAN PLOTS: Plays from central and eastern europe ed. Cheryl
Robson ISBN 0-9536757-3-4 £9.99

CLASSIC PLAYS BY WOMEN: FROM 1600 -2000 ed. Susan Croft
ISBN 978-1-906582-00-5 £16.99

VOTES FOR WOMEN AND OTHER PLAYS ed. Susan Croft
ISBN 978-1-906582-01-2 £12.99

PLAYS FOR YOUTH THEATRES AND LARGE CASTS by Neil Duffield
ISBN 978-19065820-6-7 £12.99

THEATRE CENTRE: PLAYS FOR YOUNG PEOPLE Selected and
introduced by Rosamunde Hutt ISBN 0-9542330-5-0 £12.99

PLAYS FOR YOUNG PEOPLE by Charles Way
ISBN 0-9536757-1-8 £9.99

www.aurorametro.com